RICHARD ATTENBOROUGH

To Sabrina
with love,
Richard A

RICHARD ATTENBOROUGH

NEW EDITION

David Robinson

 British Film Institute

This new edition first published in 2003 by the
BRITISH FILM INSTITUTE
21 Stephen Street, London W1T 1LN

The British Film Institute is the UK national agency with responsibility for encouraging
the arts of film and television and conserving them in the national interest.

First Edition published 1992

Cover design by Cosima Dinkel/British Film Institute
Cover photograph of Sir Richard Attenborough, 2002,
taken by Tim Clarke, Express Newspapers
Photographs on pages ii, vi, 11–15, 18–20, 22, 31, 32 & 38 from the personal collection
of Sir Richard Attenborough. Illustrations on pages 18, 19 & 22 (top) from the collection
of Roy Waters. Other photographs courtesy of BFI Stills, Posters and Designs

Pages designed and set by Ketchup, London
Printed in the UK by Cromwell Press, Trowbridge, Wiltshire

British Library Cataloguing-in-Publication Data
A catalogue record for this book is available from the British Library

ISBN 0–85170–995–8

CONTENTS

Introduction 1

Family Formation 10

Theatre Work 15

Acting in Films 24

'Actor–Manager' 29

Oh! What a Lovely War 36

Young Winston 43

A Bridge Too Far 48

Magic 55

Gandhi 60

A Chorus Line 69

Cry Freedom 74

Chaplin 83

Before the Cameras Again 91

Shadowlands and Screen Acting 94

In Love and War 99

Grey Owl 102

What Next? 106

Notes 109

Chronology 111

Filmography 116

… a small, bald, bespectacled figure who has walked with crowds and kept his virtue and talked with kings without losing the common touch, an astute politician with a steely sense of destiny, yet renowned for his modesty and revered by his followers as an almost saintly person.

Philip French, reviewing *Gandhi*, *The Observer*, 1982

… that far more subtle and often more complex courage – moral courage, such as the courage of a member of the British Establishment stepping constantly out of the hallowed bounds of that Establishment to expose the most controversial evils – and what is more, to succeed.

Donald Woods, 'Filming With Attenborough', 1987

He still takes the same size in hats. He has the same friendly, unassuming manner which made him so popular in the Scouts.

Leicester Mercury, 5 August 1942

Attenborough, *c.* 1935

INTRODUCTION

It is sometimes hard to believe that Richard Attenborough is true. He seems to be everywhere, and doing everything. It seems impossible that any one man could accomplish such a range and extent of activities – certainly that he could do them seriously or well. Attenborough in fact does most things not just conscientiously but superlatively. He will generally not even undertake them without the prior conviction that he can do so.

Looking back over his life and career, you find that he has hardly changed in his eight decades. He owes his formation to a remarkable family in which responsibility, social service, sense of community were not seen as a duty or an onerous obligation, but simply as the natural and most fulfilling way of spending your life.

This attitude has definitively shaped his thinking and life, creative as well as social. Public life is a natural obligation. His working colleagues in the cinema, exasperated at the endless outside demands on his time, call him 'The Chairman of London'. He is Chancellor of the University of Sussex and President, inter alia, of the Royal Academy of Dramatic Art, the British Academy of Film and Television Arts, the British Screen Advisory Council, the National Film and Television School, the Combined Theatrical Charities, Capital Radio, The Actors' Charitable Trust, the Gandhi Foundation, the Muscular Dystrophy Group of Great Britain, and Life Vice President of Chelsea Football Club. What is remarkable is that he is never merely a figure-head. In every case he is the most active, aware, participatory of chairmen, positively guiding whatever organisation it may be.

To an outsider, reading the formidable list in *Who's Who*, to undertake so many offices might seem at best reckless or at worst vanity and an immoderate thirst for influence. It is nothing of the sort. Attenborough accepts the positions thrust on him not because he seeks or especially enjoys them, but because unselfconsciously he knows he will be more effective than anyone else – because of his experience, his influence, his contacts and his organisational and diplomatic skills. And this implies a responsibility which he is constitutionally unable to shirk.

The sheer energy which enables him to fulfil so many functions is something that cannot be explained, though his skill in organising that energy is apparent. He deploys his forces by compartmentalising his concentration. He is able to shift the focus of his attention with astounding speed – using the time between setups on a difficult scene for a production meeting, an interview or to deal with some knotty problem of RADA, BAFTA or Denville Hall, the home for veteran actors and actresses. Having refocussed his attention in this way, his concentration on the immediate issue is total, undeflectable, unhurried, briefly but exactly scheduled before the next demand. His attention to detail – the phrasing of a document or the layout of a title – is meticulous. To administrate and service this phenomenal activity, he needs and has built up a personal staff who have learned to live with the speed and volatility of his activity and his demands for undeviating, perfect efficiency.

A Bridge Too Far (1977). Edward Fox as General Horrocks at the head of the XX Corps

Attenborough's family background was academic; and after sixty years and a considerable collection of honorary degrees he still has a vague guilty regret as the only one who did not go to university. He still, quite unreasonably, perceives this as a lack of education: he will for example say that he 'did not feel intellectually equal' to taking on direction of the National Theatre. In fact his intellectual equipment – his sense of argument and logic and analysis – is as formidable as his energy. His business partner Diana Hawkins says, 'You can persuade Dick of anything if you can persuade him with logic.'

He has a huge knowledge of all the arts: 'paintings, sculpture, the plastic arts in general occupy my life to a great degree'. He absorbs the daily papers: his politics – humanist radicalism quite opposed to any popular image of him as a pillar of the Establishment – are passionate. His memory is prodigious. He recalls precisely conversations from years back; and will remonstrate plaintively with those of feebler recollection, 'But I told you that darling. You must remember.'

He appears, remarkably, never to have been much different. In his twenties and the early years of his career, interviewers were amazed at the range of his activities – then he would be rushing from the film set to perform in the theatre, between times fitting in charity meetings and interviews. More than fifty years ago he was, as today, campaigning for every worthy cause in sight, fund-raising for RADA, involved in entertainment industry politics. The late forties were a period of upheavals in the British film industry; and Attenborough was already a spokesman. His statement at a critical meeting of Equity in 1948 was reported throughout the press. At the next meeting he was elected to chair the debate.

His championing of the art of the cinema and British cinema in particular has not altered. A public statement in 1949 is hardly different from the causes he is fighting in the 21st century – a sad and sobering reflection on the history of films in Britain: 'Mr Attenborough said that it would be a good idea to have this national cinema, so that films accepted as of artistic and cultural merit might be shown as long as the public wanted them. It would also afford the independent producer a chance to show his films. The monopoly of big film distributors was forcing the independent producer out of a fair showing. If the Government did not come to a decision quickly, the film industry would be stifled.'[1]

With Kim Stanley in
*Seance on a Wet
Afternoon* (1964)

His bewilderingly varied public life, enough for several men, together
with the familiar public image – relaxed and affable, with all the
legendary caressing and kissing and 'darlings' – tempts people to take his
creative work less seriously than it deserves. Yet the acting career alone
would stand as a life's achievement. From his first dazzling major success
in the theatre as the sinister Pinkie in *Brighton Rock*, to the screen
performances in *Seance on a Wet Afternoon*, *Guns at Batasi*, *10 Rillington
Place*, his treasurable song-and-dance bit in *Dr Dolittle* and his Kriss
Kringle in the otherwise forgettable *Miracle on 34th Street*, he has been
without question one of the most resourceful and intelligent British
actors of his time, on stage and screen.

His true vocation, he says is as actor–manager; and from 1960 he
became a producer. With growing freedom to choose his subjects, he told
an interviewer in 1963, 'I'm not interested in detective stories or love
stories. I'm fascinated by figures who have changed, and who still are
changing, our society.'[2] Later statements of intention include: 'The cinema
as an end in itself is not enough. It cannot afford to be narcissistic'; 'I
wish to make a plea to the strong for the weak.'[3]

The subject and what he has to communicate are paramount for Attenborough. The essential subject is very often his own intense feeling for the character – whether it be Gandhi, Chaplin or the desperate hopefuls in *A Chorus Line*. A special appeal of his films is his ability to communicate very directly his intense personal affection for his characters. 'That's what I mean when I say sometimes that I'm a boring director. I don't use film in the way that the great auteurs do. I use film, the camera, to record as effectively and as perceptively as I am able what I want to say through the actors. In *A Chorus Line*, if that didn't work with the kids – my feeling for them – there was no movie. Each of them at any one time took over the screen.'[4] As a producer–director, Attenborough meticulously pre-plans his films (whenever possible with the skilful logistical aid of his regular production collaborator Terence Clegg and co-producer Diana Hawkins) and shoots as far as possible to exact schedule. 'I am always conscious that the funding I ultimately acquire is in some degree high risk. Most of my films do not really conform to ordinary commercial requirements. Biographies are not a financially seductive subject matter, and rarely do well. So I am very aware of my obligations to that painfully acquired funding. Out of a sort

With John Leyton and Mia Farrow in *Guns at Batasi* (1964)

of boy scout sense of honour, I feel that I must do everything in my power to husband those funds as responsibly and professionally as I can. When I am making a film I dare not fall behind schedule. I dare not find myself in a position where funds which are finite are used in anything but the best possible way, to put the maximum on the screen.

'So I always think ahead and prepare meticulously. I can scarcely ever remember going on to a set not prepared, knowing what I want to do. Unless, that is, I have – very rarely – woken up and realised that my ideas for that day are terrible.

'In some degree too this comes from an actor's discipline. You can never appear unprepared. You cannot step onto the stage and not know what you are going to do.'

Attenborough constantly deprecates himself as 'a boring director'; and a lot of critics have seen fit to corroborate his view in writing about what may seem like stately, occasional epics. 'My style is preconceived and, therefore, I think it's sometimes a bit mundane. If I am self-critical, I have to say that I think my work tends perhaps to be over-formulated. I sometimes wish that I'd been a bit more unconventional – flamboyant almost.'[5]

It is an underestimation. Attenborough – very visibly in his work on the set – is wholly creative. True, his sort of creativity can all too easily be blurred in the kind of big-budget pictures in which he works. Films of that cost must be formally framed with the guarantees of stars, beautiful sets, highly polished photography and sound and technique. There is little room for improvisational invention. The obligatory industrial conventions of master-shot and coverage impose certain conventions on the editing. If Attenborough's career ever permitted him to make a film under the more constricting financial conditions of European production, his creativity might well be more fully visible.

Foremost is his skill with actors. He cherishes and caresses them, literally and figuratively. He is prepared to discuss and prepare a role as much or as little as the actor wishes or needs; and can appear endlessly patient with the most garrulous self-analytical performer. On the set too he assesses at every moment the degree of help the actor wants. He reassures them with compliments like 'Well played, darling!'[6]

Film acting, he feels, makes much greater demands than the stage:

'You go on to the set and probably you've had no rehearsals – possibly some discussions with the director – and suddenly a hundred and fifty people, and lights and God knows whatall are focussed on you. And you have to offer up whatever you've got. So you're nervous. You're terrified sometimes. You're inhibited, embarrassed. Nine times out of ten the chances are that unless the director can do something about that, you're going to fall back on technique and tricks, and things you've done in previous performances. You don't relax as an actor – and if you don't relax, you don't venture.

'If the director is unable to do something about it, he's going to get an ordinary performance. So to that extent I think an actor directing has a head start on directors who don't understand that. The most essential thing, I believe, that a director's got to do – is to convince the actor or actress that he or she is the one player in Christendom who should be playing this part, and who will play it better than anybody else possibly could.

'If you can do that, then the little proportion of the actor's mind that stands outside and has a look at what he's doing is reduced to the absolute minimum. Technique and tricks are reduced to a negligible factor. And being – actually being – becomes the performance, rather than performing.'[7]

His skill in casting is also the outcome of his own years as an actor. 'Casting is very much a directorial skill.' The choice of actors for the main roles in his films is never obvious. In the title roles of *Young Winston*, *Gandhi* and *Chaplin* – parts as demanding and vital to the success of the film as any in the cinema – he boldly cast actors who had never had leading film roles. 'Nobody was sure of Robert Downey Jr; but for me there was no question of the potential in him – even if his Hollywood roles had never to any real extent plumbed that talent.'

The same skill and certainty extends to matching major stars to small but telling roles (Attenborough's personal standing, not to speak of his charm, can win anyone to work with him.) He is no less diligent in casting walk-on and non-speaking parts. At auditions he is unfailingly courteous, hates to disappoint any applicant, and will sometimes invent a niche for a particularly promising unknown. His own success has made him more rather than less sensitive; and the most modest actors are swept off their feet by his charm and courtesy at what for other directors or casting directors would be 'cattle calls'. 'Auditions are terrible. People can be so humiliated. I was so lucky because I never had to go through that.' 'Being an actor, one is conscious of just what auditions, in any form, mean to the person concerned. If you are offering your painting or your book, that is an article which is either accepted or rejected. If you are auditioning as a performer, you undergo personal acceptance or rejection.'[8] He recalls a persistent and volatile young dancer who appeared at the *A Chorus Line* auditions. Finally rejected, 'tears coursed down her cheeks, and, grabbing her dance bag from a chair, she careered out of the studio door. I followed her, terrified she'd run under a car …'[9]

Despite his fears of 'dullness' Attenborough possesses – perhaps in part derived from his stage training – a strong sense of mise-en-scène and mise-en-shot. This was pre-eminently demonstrated in his first film as director *Oh! What a Lovely War*. (Significantly, perhaps, this was his

Attenborough as Albert Blossom with Rex Harrison as Dolittle in *Dr Dolittle* (1967)

most modestly budgeted film.) His powerful sense of the dramatic geography of a scene is often seen more strongly in the first 'master shot' than in the finished cut scene. He works with story-boards; but his story-board artists are often frustrated to find that Attenborough wants their designs as a spring-board, against which to react.

As producer-director, an outstanding asset is his quality of leadership. He has a singular gift for maintaining the morale of a unit. No matter what administrative problems may irritate him in the privacy of his trailer, on set he radiates confidence and good humour. The first that is heard from him on set in the morning is generally laughter, as if there were a script direction, 'enter, laughing'. He jokes with everyone and the toughest labourer is unembarrassed when addressed as 'Poppy' or 'Darling'. He knows every last assistant, painter and grip by name; and is unfailingly courteous to them all. Extras are addressed as 'Sir' and 'Madam'. The style pays off better than the bullying of martinets. Not that Attenborough is less than an autocrat to his unit; but he rules by expectation. He takes for granted the total loyalty and dedication of his collaborators, and gives them no less in return. To disappoint that trust and expectation would seem unthinkable.

The ultimate style and effect of Attenborough's films depends upon the balance between his passion to communicate, his unembarrassed will to heighten social consciousness in his public, and his sheer joy in entertaining. Effective communication – as well as commercial viability – always means winning the largest audience. He often says, 'I am not interested in making films for two men and a dog in a barn. And I don't want to preach to the converted.' In 1991 (instancing mega-budgets of that period) he declared, 'I don't compromise – but it's a fine line. I've never put in a character, or dialogue, or changed anything that I've wanted to say as a concession merely to obtain funds. But I envisage the concept of the picture, right from the word go, to appeal to a world market so as to recoup the budget. I could make the most marvellously self-indulgent film for $30 million. But because it would only gross $2 million, I would never work again. Since there are subjects that I'm bursting to make, I have to try and make viable films.'[10]

'In some quarters "popularise" is a dirty word. But it is a banner under which I will gladly sail.'[11]

FAMILY FORMATION

A journalist of the 1990s wrote that Richard Attenborough had spent his life trying to live up to his father. He intended to be mean; but Attenborough took it as a compliment which could only have been more welcome if the writer had added 'and his mother'. Few men can ever have been, to the extent that Attenborough is, the product of their family environment.

Attenborough remembers only happiness from his childhood in a comfortable middle-class home and an inter-war provincial society that, even after the First World War, still had some quality of the Edwardian. What was exceptional in the family was the energy of his parents' sense of practical idealism and human service.

His father, Frederick Attenborough, was born in Stapleford, Nottinghamshire, the son of the village baker. From school he won his way to Bangor Teacher Training College. He went to work as a school-teacher in Liverpool, but then won a foundation scholarship to Emmanuel College Cambridge, where he eventually became a don. In 1925 he was appointed Principal of Borough Road Training College, Isleworth (now West London Institute of Higher Education), and finally in 1932, when Richard was nine, became principal of University College, Leicester. He remained there until his retirement in 1951, having piloted the college to full university status.

An important influence upon Frederick Attenborough's early educational aspirations was his schoolmaster Samuel Clegg, whose daughter Mary was eventually to become his wife. Clegg was an educationalist of distinction, who also wrote a number of books on art appreciation.

Frederick's favourite recreations were music and photography: he

Richard and his mother,
photographed by his
father, 1923

contributed to the King Penguin series of monographs a charming book
of photographs, with a commentary by Niklaus Pevsner, *The Leaves of
Southwell* (1945). He also passed on to his sons a passion for football (a
boyhood football injury had prevented him from serving in the First
World War).

Richard, born in Cambridge on 29 August 1923, was exposed to
culture early and easily. His parents and grandparents were all musical,
and he has a very early impression of hearing *Messiah* conducted by Dr
Malcolm Sargent in the De Montfort Hall, Leicester. Samuel Clegg
would show him picture books of great paintings and explain them to
him. As he grew older he was accustomed to meeting socially and affa-
bly the celebrities who were from time to time entertained at the college:
he recalls they included Jan Masaryk, Sir Hugh Roberton (founder and
conductor of the Glasgow Orpheus Choir), Sir Thomas Beecham, Sir
Stafford Cripps, Matheson Lang, Mary Jarred, Eric Gill, Reynolds Stone
and Dilys Powell. He also recalls delightful friendships struck up with
cockney workmen, who enriched his vocabulary beyond the range of
polite drawing room conversation.

Above all, though, Richard and his two younger brothers, David and
John, were brought up with a very practical sense of social responsibili-
ties. 'Mary and the Governor felt unquestionably that in order to enjoy

Richard Attenborough in
1926, photographed by
his father

living to the full, you simply had to be conscious of others and their
quality of life. It followed that you should be prepared to make some
sort of sacrifice – and I don't mean that in an over-moral sense – wher-
ever it was possible to help.'[12] As children they took their out-grown
clothes to homes in the 'working class' parts of Leicester impoverished
by Depression. On their annual holiday in Wales, the Attenboroughs
always took with them boys from the housing estates, who would otherwise never see the sea.

During the Spanish Civil War Mary Attenborough was chairman of a
committee to care for evacuee Basque children. She also took part in a
protest against the bombardment of Guernica, marching alongside the
local Communist leader – which resulted in a brick through the
Attenborough's drawing room window.

In the thirties Frederick Attenborough chaired a committee to bring
Jewish refugees out of Germany. Some stayed with the family. On the
outbreak of war the Attenboroughs took two Jewish girls into their
home, where they were adopted as sisters to the boys and stayed for
eight years. 'That particular decision, not merely paying lip service but
taking positive, responsible action to help other human beings, made a
profound impression on me. It has, I suppose, affected my life and my
attitudes ever since.'[13]

People who remember Mrs Attenborough say that it is from her that Richard inherits his energy and non-stop activity. When she died, crashing her car after apparently suffering a heart attack, she was returning alone from a committee meeting in the early hours of the morning. Her death was the greatest sorrow the family ever suffered; and Frederick Attenborough, who survived her by twelve years, never recovered from it.

Richard recalls that the dramatic instinct came early, again no doubt inherited from his mother, who was president of an active amateur company, the Leicester Little Theatre. (Subsequently Richard was to become the theatre's honorary Life President.) Frederick Attenborough too may have had some secret theatrical ambitions: a photograph from 1907 shows him as the Duke in a production of *The Merchant of Venice*. Richard remembers his own first appearance in the school dramatic society as a fairy in *Iolanthe*; and in 1931, at eight, he took over at short notice and to great applause a role in the 9th Leicester Cubs' production of *A Tight Corner*. Talents as impresario emerged at 12, when he mounted a variety show in the local church hall. By agreeing to donate any profits to the Society for the

Frederick Attenborough as an amateur actor in 1907 – as the Duke in *The Merchant of Venice*

The St Barnabas Hall concert, 1935. Richard and David Attenborough as two charladies

Attenborough family group, 1943. In front, Frederick and Mary Attenborough; behind, David, Sheila Sim (just engaged to RA), John and Richard

Prevention of Cruelty to Animals he secured the cooperation of his brother David, whose own life interests were already determined. The brothers performed a comic duet, 'Ladies Wot Come To Oblige', dressed as charladies. Their parents came as members of the audience. Richard bounced up on stage half way through the show to announce that there would now be a 20-minute interval, but was mortified when his father called out 'Nonsense, Richard. Ten minutes is quite enough.'

After more mature experience with the Leicester Little Theatre, he was convinced that he wanted to be an actor. His father, already disappointed in his son's lack of application at school, Wyggeston Grammar, reluctantly agreed that he might go to the Royal Academy of Dramatic Art, but only on condition that he could win a scholarship. With the help of the director of Leicester Little Theatre, Richard studied his audition pieces, speeches from de Stogumber in Shaw's *St Joan* and Ormerod the bibulous photographer in J. B. Priestley's *When We Are Married*.

The examiners included the veteran actors Athene Seyler and Felix Aylmer. Attenborough was selected for RADA's only competitive award, the Leverhulme Scholarship. This covered tuition fees and also carried an allowance of £2.10s a week. So in 1941 Attenborough moved to London, where he stayed with his favourite aunt in Wimbledon and cycled to the Academy every day to save money.

Summing up his youth, he recalled in 1982, 'The family home, if I choose one impression that overrides all others, was continually full of laughter. There was always masses going on – people coming and going – but essentially it was a place of joy. The Governor was a marvellous raconteur and his sense of humour and ability to communicate his own excitement and involvement in everything around him has, I believe stood both Dave and me in very good stead.'[14]

THEATRE WORK

S uccess came almost instantly to Attenborough, and was to last. Perhaps his greatest achievement was to survive this early success unscathed and unspoiled – as interviewers have been noting, with ever new surprise and delight, for the past sixty years. He arrived at RADA for the autumn term of 1940.

During the 1941 summer vacation he was invited by Ronald Kerr, a theatre director who taught at RADA, to play the part of Richard Miller in a production of Eugene O'Neill's *Ah, Wilderness!* at the Intimate Theatre, Palmer's Green. He also had roles in *Cottage to Let* and *Goodbye, Mr Chips*. A fellow cast-member of *Ah, Wilderness!*, Peggy Cummings, had as her agent the American-born Al Parker. Originally an

Class at RADA, 1942: RA standing far left. Sheila Sim is the central figure, with the actor Harold Lang standing to her right. In the wartime period the girls outnumbered the boys. The actor at the far right is Wolfe Morris

In Which We Serve
(1942). Attenborough
makes his screen debut
as a frightened stoker

actor, Parker became a Hollywood director in 1916 (he made three films
with Douglas Fairbanks) before arriving in Britain in 1932 to make 'quota
quickies'. Late in the 1930s he set up his theatrical agency in London.
Parker saw *Ah, Wilderness!* and offered to take Richard on as a client.

Parker quickly found Attenborough his first film role in Noel
Coward's *In Which We Serve*. But at this time his future seemed to be the
stage; and Parker plotted his theatrical career sagely. After finishing *In
Which We Serve* Attenborough appeared in the RADA public show of *The
Lady With the Lamp*, and won the Bancroft Silver Medal for his perform-
ance. On the strength of this he was offered an understudy part in the
West End, the newspaper reporter in the Haymarket production of *The
Doctor's Dilemma*, with Vivien Leigh. To his disappointment, Al Parker –
concerned enough to travel to Leicester to discuss it with the family –
counselled him not to take it: with only seven months before call-up,
Parker said, it would be a waste of the time to tie himself up in a long-
running play, rather than getting experience and notice in a variety of jobs.

Parker's wisdom was vindicated when Attenborough was given his first West End part in Clifford Odets' *Awake and Sing*, which opened at the Arts Theatre on 20 May and transferred to the Cambridge Theatre on 4 August. The play was presented by the Arts Theatre Group of Actors and directed by Alec Clunes. Attenborough played Ralph, the younger son of a Bronx Jewish family, a character described in the programme notes as 'a boy with a clean spirit. He wants to know, wants to learn. He is ardent, he is romantic, he is sensitive. He is naif too. He is trying to find out why so much dirt must be cleared away before it is possible to "get to first base".' *The Times* said the role was played 'with sound understanding'. *The Daily Sketch* opinion that 'Richard Attenborough shows an intensity of feeling and restraint for a youngster who has a big future', was used in the publicity.

A biographical note in the programme explained that 'Owing to the calling-up of another actor, who was to have played the part originally in *Awake and Sing*, eighteen-year-old Richard Attenborough got his first part in London's West End … Richard, when not acting in *Awake and Sing*, has a special hobby, which is to go and see as many films and plays as he possibly can.'

Other roles at the Arts Theatre included Sebastian in *Twelfth Night*, opposite Jean Forbes Robertson, and Ba in James Bridie's *Holy Isle*. As the country boy in the Arts' Christmas production of *Maria Marten or the Murder in the Red Barn* he sang a duet with Joan Gates which was featured by *Picture Post* as 'the hit of the show'.

At RADA he met and fell in love with a fellow student, Sheila Sim – they were to marry on 22 January 1945. On 1 September 1942 they appeared on stage together for the first time in Aimée Stuart's play *London W1* at the Q Theatre, with the character names Penny and Andrew.

In October Attenborough played Leo Hubbard in the first London production of *The Little Foxes*, directed by Emlyn Williams at the Piccadilly Theatre. The cast included Fay Compton and the veteran black entertainer Connie Smith. Barely half a year after leaving RADA, Attenborough was already in demand both as actor and celebrity. In January 1943 his performance in a radio adaptation of Hans Andersen's *The Garden of Paradise* drew a revealing commentary from C. Gordon Glover, writing in *The Radio Times*: 'Attenborough, fresh from R.A.D.A., where he won the Bancroft Silver Medal, is nineteen years old and prodigiously capable. He has already appeared in four West End plays and seems to be sure of early stardom – he scored a tremendous success as the young stoker in Coward's film *In Which We Serve.* I wish him very well, for he has all the bright and shining energies of youth, and is a very pleasant young man indeed.'

Already busy with public appearances, in January 1943 he was a judge in the Miss Watford of 1943 contest. In March he was back in Watford Town Hall with Michael Redgrave and James Agate, adjudicating a 'Miss England' contest. (The winner was a 20-year-old Civil Defence ambulance driver, Maureen Boles.)

The same month saw his biggest stage success, rocketing him to national stardom. *Brighton Rock,* adapted by Frank Harvey from Grahame Greene's novel, opened on tour at the Bristol Hippodrome on 22 February 1943. The play was produced by Richard Bird, and the cast also included Hermione Baddeley, Dulcie Gray, Harcourt Williams and William Hartnell. The following week in Oxford the critic of *The Oxford Mail* wrote, 'Mr Richard Attenborough certainly stands, on the strength of this performance alone, as one of our most powerful actors.

Theatre World, April 1943 – spotlight on the stage version of *Brighton Rock*

'A mere child in appearance (in age, too, if it comes to that) there is nothing immature about his technique, which bears comparison with such a veteran as Harcourt Williams. It is a performance of which Charles Laughton might well be proud.' The critic had praise too for another new young member of the cast, Dulcie Gray.

There was a shrewd review in *The Oxford Magazine* by an 18-year-old undergraduate who was to make his own mark in the theatre – Peter Brook. He found the characters 'astonishingly well observed, especially the crowd of minor characters – tourists, tarts, invalids, fishermen, and maiden ladies – who ceaselessly pass to and fro.' The weakness he felt was the ending: 'a play that sets out to present a realistic chunk of life should not artificially round up its action at the end of three acts. Real life has no final curtains, and there the conclusion should have been left open.' Of the actors, 'the greatest praise must go to Richard Attenborough for a first-rate performance as Pinkie, although he is a trifle too melodramatic, and to Dulcie Gray for a really outstanding piece of action.'

When the play came into London on 11 March 1943, the press was unanimous in its enthusiasm and predictions of stardom for both Attenborough and Dulcie Gray. Only *The Times* was somewhat stuffy, finding the play's violence distasteful and regretting that 'If Mr Richard Attenborough, who, as the gangster leader Pinkie has an even more unpleasant role than that which he had recently in *The Little Foxes*, is going to be typed so early in his career, the ability which won for him a high award at the R.A.D.A. only a year ago seems well on the way to being stifled before it comes to maturity. This young man's capabilities and talents could assuredly be shown to equal advantage in less unpleasant characterisations, and he should not be allowed to get into the rut of villainous and degenerate parts.' Much more typical of the notices was the *New Statesman and Nation*, which said that Attenborough 'deserves to have won fame in a single night, for his study in abnormal psychology is thoughtful, delicate and powerful'.

The most enigmatic compliment however came, though not in print, from the feared doyen of London theatre critics James Agate. Unprecedentedly, he came round to Attenborough's dressing room after the performance, marched in, and announced, 'Young man, I never make a practice of coming round to actors' dressing rooms. I consider you are in danger of becoming a great actor. I therefore never wish to see you again.' 'It was extraordinary', Attenborough remembers, 'because of course he was God. I don't know what he meant by it – a ridiculous theatrical gesture. But I can still see him as clear as day. He hardly came into the door. A funny little man, with a stick with an ivory knob. It was unbelievable. James Agate!'

The run of *Brighton Rock* came to a premature end after 100 performances, when Attenborough was called into the Royal Air Force. However he was to make a few wartime stage appearances which do not figure in his official curriculum vitae. On Sunday 9 May 1943 he took

GARRICK THEATRE
Licensed by the Lord Chamberlain to D. A. Abrahams
CHARING CROSS ROAD, LONDON, W.C.2

EVENINGS at 6 p.m.
MATINEES:
Wednesday and Saturday at 2.30

LINNIT & DUNFEE LTD.
By arrangement with Carlnej Productions, Ltd.

present

HERMIONE BADDELEY

in

"BRIGHTON ROCK" 6ᴰ·

Adapted from the Book by
GRAHAM GREENE

By FRANK HARVEY
(*Author of "Saloon Bar"*)

PROGRAMME

THE MAGAZINE PROGRAMME
Owing to the paper restrictions order, we are compelled to suspend our usual Magazine features, but they will be resumed as soon as normal publication becomes possible.
Grantley & Co., Ltd., 63/65, Piccadilly, London, W.1.

Programme for the original London production of *Brighton Rock*: clearly prepared before the young Attenborough's dominance had become evident part in a special 'Tribute to the Fighting Women of Great Britain and Czechoslovakia'. His role was alongside Wendy Hiller in a one-act play, *Mothers Are Waiting*, directed by a young Czech emigré, Herbert Lom.

For a week in September 1943 he appeared at the Arts Theatre Cambridge in *Men in Shadow*, by Mary Hayley Bell, the wife of John Mills who had appeared in the original London production. He was billed as 'AC2 Attenborough, appearing by courtesy of Officer Commanding No 2 I.T.W. RAF'. The publicity promised that 'The production of *Men in Shadow* will enable Cambridge audiences to see the greatest young actor of the English Stage, Richard Attenborough, as "Lew Messinger" a role already made famous during the long run of the London production at the Vaudeville Theatre by John Mills.' Attenborough was still only a year and a half out of RADA.

In 1944 he was seconded to the RAF Film Unit, stationed at Pinewood Studios. This period brought encounters which he still reckons as high points of his experience. One was working in the cutting room of Humphrey Jennings, the surrealist painter and Britain's greatest documentary film-maker and cinema poet. Another was acting alongside Edward G. Robinson and Bessie Love in *Journey Together*, a propaganda production scripted by Terence Rattigan. Sheila Sim, who had just become engaged to Attenborough, also acted for the film, but her part was cut out during editing. The film's director, John Boulting, was to become the young Attenborough's closest friend; and

John, Richard and David
Attenborough in 1944

Attenborough still contends that Boulting taught him more about film acting than any other director. Attenborough's role in *Journey Together*, as a would-be pilot who has to be content to be a navigator, to an extent reflected the frustration of his own ambitions to be a pilot, as a result of his secondment to the RAF Film Unit. He did however get some flying experience before the war ended, as a trainee air gunner.

Attenborough and Sheila Sim personally presented *Journey Together* when it was shown in his home town, Leicester. He 'thanked the audience for their kind reception, and said he must hand the credit to the RAF for the picture had been made by the RAF Film production unit, and showed actual personnel. He eulogised Edward G. Robinson, both as actor and man at work. The American star had given his services free for the making of the film.' ('How could I refuse?' Attenborough remembers Robinson saying. 'I am a Jew!')

The critics were unanimous in their enthusiasm for Attenborough: a *Daily Despatch* writer announced that 'Britain's first post-war star was "born" yesterday'. The film also brought his earliest American reviews. Bosley Crowther, the august and severe critic of the *New York Times*, evidently thought he was a non-professional: 'It is no reflexion on Mr Robinson and Miss Love … to say that the actual airmen are much more creditable in this film than they are. Richard Attenborough, who plays the principal trainee, is a thoroughly engaging lad, combining a boyish talent for humor with a fine tone of sincerity.'

In 1946 he was demobilised; and on January 1946 took part in a radio adaptation of *The Way to the Stars*, with Celia Johnson. He returned to the West End stage as Coney, in Arthur Laurents' *Home of the Brave*, directed by Joel O'Brien. The pre-London tour took him back home, to the Opera House, Leicester, and the play opened at the Westminster Theatre, under a new title, *The Way Back*, on 27 January 1949. Attenborough played a Jewish G.I. suffering from severe mental disturbance. The action of the play involves his recovery in the care of a sensitive psychiatrist, with flashbacks to his war experience. The play was also perceived by the critics as an attack on anti-Semitism. By now it was predictable that however mixed the opinions of any production in which the young Attenborough appeared, praise for his performance would be unanimous. At a special midnight performance of *The Way Back* for the profession, he was given an ovation and a special tribute from Laurence Olivier.

In 1949 he told a reporter that he would love to find a play for himself and Sheila, so that they could work as a stage couple, as Michael Denison and Dulcie Gray were doing, 'but if we found a play we would probably never get a theatre'.[15] He was wrong. On 23 November 1950 they opened together at the Savoy in Roger MacDougall's farce *To Dorothy, a Son*, starring Yolande Donlan. The production transferred the following year to the Garrick and ran for 514 performances. Attenborough's next play, Peter Jones' comedy *Sweet Madness* had a shorter run, despite a change of title: on tour it was improbably called *Song of the Centipede*.

Richard Attenborough and Sheila Sim were again teamed, in a play which was to be a theatrical phenomenon, breaking every theatrical record in the world. After a pre-London tour *The Mousetrap* opened at the Ambassadors Theatre on 25 November 1952. More than fifty years later it is still running.

'We were terribly lucky. This was the age of film stars. Forty years ago there were no pop stars or television stars. In those days when we went to the annual *Sunday Pictorial* Film Garden Party we needed the sort of protection that Michael Jackson gets now. Our generation were the last of those movie stars whom the public wanted to see and follow around.

'When we took *The Mousetrap* out on tour we never had an empty seat. At the Opera House Manchester, with 2000 seats, you couldn't get a ticket for a matinée. We were movie stars, going out into the theatre – which not many of them did. We had this extraordinary circumstance whereby the play was in profit long before it came into London.

'I remember walking round our garden with the late Peter Saunders, the play's impresario, trying to decide whether we should go into the Winter Garden or the Ambassadors. We had to decide before we went on tour because the sets had to be built in advance, and the Winter Garden stage was more than twice the size of the Ambassadors'.

'We were apprehensive. We didn't know what it would do in London – even though Agatha Christie prophesied, 'We should get a nice little run out of it'.

'Contrary to the legend that has grown up, it did not get

The Mousetrap (1952).
Richard Attenborough
and Sheila Sim

bad reviews. In fact it had some very good reviews indeed, and from serious critics.

'We settled on the Ambassadors, because we felt it was rather a miniature work. The result of that was that Sheila and I said to Peter, 'We can't manage on the percentages we will get at such a small theatre. May we invest?' He not only allowed us to invest, but did not even ask us to put up cash – he took the money from our tour percentages. Thus we owned ten per cent of the longest- running play in history. The play was a success from the start, with good reviews, two movie stars, and the greatest box office asset of all, Mrs Christie. There were queues every day. Whilst Sheila and I were in the play there was never, on any occasion, an empty seat.

'*The Mousetrap* – and Peter Saunders' friendship and generosity – eventually helped me to make *Gandhi*. When I needed to find money to develop it, Peter bought back my shares on very generous terms.'

By the time Attenborough ended his two-year run in *The Mousetrap*, it was clear that his destiny was now the cinema. He had already made a score of films and been a star for a decade.

There were two final stage appearances. In November 1956 he appeared with Sheila Sim in *Double Image* by Roger MacDougall and Ted Allan. It opened at the Savoy but transferred early in the following year to the St James, presented by Laurence Olivier, who owned the theatre. It was the final production at the 120-year-old theatre, which was demolished, amid mourning and protests in which the Attenboroughs, inevitably, were prominent.

His final stage appearance to date was as Theseus in Benn W. Levy's *The Rape of the Belt* (Piccadilly Theatre, 12 December 1957). The production, directed by John Clements, and also starring Clements, Constance Cummings and Kay Hammond, ran for 298 performances.

'I would have liked to do more theatre. The trouble is that theatre is expensive today. If you go into a commercial production, you must stay in it for six months or a year. Or you hope to be invited to play in one of the national companies, but that means that it would be impossible to direct a movie at the same time. Maybe towards the end of my days it would be nice to play a Lionel Barrymore part in a wheel chair, but someone, of course, would have to ask me. My son Michael has taken over direction of the Almeida Theatre – maybe he'll offer me a chance one day!'

ACTING IN FILMS

A ttenborough's earliest surviving professional press notice comes from *The Evening News*, 17 March 1942: 'People who spy out for young talent are talking about 18-year-old Richard Attenborough. He won a silver medal at R.A.D.A., has three film parts already offered him, and is already busy in Noel Coward's *In Which We Serve* ... there seems no stopping him now. Except, maybe, the Army; he has to register next week.'

Immediately after taking on Attenborough as client, Al Parker persuaded Noel Coward to test him for *In Which We Serve*, based on the wartime exploits of Lord Louis Mountbatten's ship HMS *Kelly*. (In the film the ship, renamed HMS *Torrin*, was recreated at Denham studios.) Attenborough was given the part – the youngest member of the crew, a frightened sailor who deserts his post. On their first meeting Coward announced to him, 'You're Rich-odd Att-en-bor-ough, aren't you? My name is Noel Coward. You are going to be very, very good in my film.'

'I remember so clearly being more frightened than I've ever been in my life on the first day that I worked on the film. That was in 1941. Thank God, I was sitting on the deck and I was supposed to be dying. I think if I'd had to move at all I would have fallen over I was so nervous. And I think that is by no means an exception. The part was tiny, but won some nice notices.' [16]

Before being called up for service in the RAF, and appearing in *Journey Together*, Attenborough also played small parts in *Schweik's New Adventures*, directed by a Czech emigré, Carl Lamac; and in Brian Desmond Hurst's *The Hundred Pound Window* (the title referred to the race-course totalisator; and the cast included Anne Crawford, Mary Clare, David Farrar and Frederick Leister).

With Jack Watling and
Edward G. Robinson,
Journey Together (1945)

During a seventy-two hour leave, he visited the set of *A Matter of Life and Death* with Sheila Sim, who had worked with Powell and Pressburger in *A Canterbury Tale*, and was by this time his wife. Attenborough made a one-shot appearance as an airman in the film, 'for which I was paid £15 – about forty times my daily seven-and-threepence in the RAF'. Following his demobilisation he played the romantic lead in one of his few costume pictures, *The Man Within*, directed by Bernard Knowles, adapted from Graham Greene's novel, and with a cast that included Michael Redgrave, Joan Greenwood and Jean Kent. Attenborough's role was as a young member of a smuggling gang who betrays the leader he has worshipped. Shown in the United States as *The Smugglers*, it drew from the *Los Angeles Times* the comment, 'So little known was the young actor playing the youth that he received almost no billing, yet it is safe to say that he will become a star. His name is Richard Attenborough.'

The 25-year-old Peter Ustinov's first film as director, *School for Secrets* – the story of the invention of radar – returned Attenborough to the fighting forces, on screen at least. Throughout the fifties and sixties, British cinema had a strong militaristic trend. Although Attenborough was only to play an RAF officer once more, in John Sturges' *The Great Escape* (1962), the naval career launched in *In Which We Serve* was extensive: *Morning Departure, The Gift Horse, The Ship That Died of*

Shame, The Baby and the Battleship, The Sand Pebbles (USA, 1966).
Milton Shulman once wrote that Attenborough and John Mills were in
so many nautical pictures that 'they will soon be walking with a list'. He
played army personnel in *Private's Progress, Sea of Sand, Danger Within,
Guns at Batasi, The Last Grenade, Conduct Unbecoming* and, finally, in
Satyajit Ray's *The Chess Players* (1977).

In John Paddy Carstairs' thriller *Dancing With Crime* (1947), he
played husband to his real-life wife, Sheila Sim. This time he was
restored to contemporary civilian life, as a willing young London taxi
driver who finds himself driving a corpse.

In 1947 he signed a contract with the Boulting Brothers. Their first
collaboration was an adaptation of his stage success, *Brighton Rock*. John
Boulting's film version was generally regarded as brilliant, though for the
taste of the time Graham Greene's story tended to be viewed as 'sordid'.
The Times felt that Attenborough was handicapped by the truncation of
the text and the character; C. A. Lejeune however thought him a 'clear,
four-dimensional figure', and the critic of *The Lady*, 'terrifyingly convincing'. 'Of course it is only the bad reviews one remembers. Leonard
Mosley wrote that I was as close to Greene's Pinkie as Donald Duck is
to Greta Garbo. That was offset by a copy of the book which I still have,
and which Greene inscribed to "The Perfect Pinkie"'.

His performance in Sidney Gilliat's *London Belongs to Me* (1948) earned from John Barber, writing in *Leader Magazine* the compliment, 'Attenborough is unique in his class – an actor who, in spite of his youth, understands human frailty.' The film had very mixed notices, but praise for Attenborough was unanimous. As *The Times* put it: 'An extremely entertaining film may evidently be made with commonplace material, and this version of Mr Norman Collins's novel owes its prime distinction to a performance by Mr Richard Attenborough.... The beauty of Mr Attenborough's performance ... is in its unsentimental statement of weakness.' The *Spectator* said that he 'mixes the ingredients of modern youth, instability, kindheartedness, carelessness for the future and complete mental wooliness with an adroit and shining spoon, and his performance can be recommended as being one of the finest we have seen for a long time'.

His second post-war film with the Boultings, *The Guinea Pig*, was based on Warren Chetham Strode's West End success (Criterion Theatre, 1946) about an educational experiment in which a boy from a humble working-class home is sent to a major public school. The social embarrassments that are the theme of the film now seem a trifle archaic, though they were very much a reality at the time: the play was actually inspired by the Flemyng Report on Education.

Attenborough's baby face was becoming a liability. Here, at 25, with hair already thinning, he was cast as a 15-year-old boy; and many of the critics commented on the fact. To add to the irony, his wife Sheila Sim played his housemistress in the film. Paul Dehn thought he had nevertheless 'considerable plausibility'; and *The Times* said: 'The mind of Mr Richard Attenborough does all it can to overcome the handicap of the body and voice too old for the part.'

Looking back, Attenborough feels that his career now hit its low point. 'There came a period where I was almost a figure of derision for the awful pictures I did and my type casting image and so on.' *The Lost People* was 'diabolical'; *Boys in Brown* – in which his fellow Borstal inmates included Dirk Bogarde, Graham Payn and Jimmy Hanley – 'pretty bad'; *Hell is Sold Out* 'unbelievably appalling'; *The Gift Horse* 'pretty boring'; *Father's Doing Fine* 'ludicrous'.

Roy Baker's *Morning Departure*, in which Attenborough plays one of four men trapped when a submarine strikes a mine, was considerably better. The release of the film coincided with an actual naval disaster, involving the submarine *Affray*; and Attenborough, predictably, was foremost in the resulting charitable appeals. He took part in the parade of British film actors in John Boulting's occasional offering for the Festival of Britain, *The Magic Box*, celebrating (and considerably exaggerating) the achievement of the British Victorian film pioneer William Friese-Greene, played by one of Attenborough's most admired actors, Robert Donat.

In the early fifties things began to look up again. He feels that Lance Comfort's *Eight O'Clock Walk* (1954), was 'all right'. The film is an anticipation of the anti-capital punishment theme of *10 Rillington Place*: Attenborough plays a likeable taxi driver who is almost convicted, wrongly, of murder, on circumstantial evidence. This was followed by the leading role in the Relph-Dearden adaptation of Nicholas Montserrat's *The Ship That Died of Shame*, directed by Basil Dearden, a director for whom he retains great respect.

In 1955 he was reunited with the Boulting Brothers, who were now moving into their most fruitful period. A series of satirical comedies at the expense of national institutions brought a new vigour to a British cinema that seemed tired and lack-lustre after the decline of Ealing. In their army comedy *Private's Progress,* Attenborough was a barrack-room lawyer and inveterate scrounger. In *Brothers in Law* he was a sharp young barrister. *I'm All Right Jack* was the last and best of the group, taking on the risky target of trades unions. Attenborough plays Sidney de Vere Cox, a munitions manufacturer supplying missiles to the Middle East.

The fifties ended with good performances in decent, forgettable films that rarely deserved him: a schoolmaster in *The Scamp*; a suburban bureaucrat who becomes a hero in *Dunkirk*; a mild, sad man who runs berserk in *The Man Upstairs*, which was produced by the Association of Cinematograph Technicians; sailor in *The Baby and the Battleship*, Desert Rat in *Sea of Sand*; army officer in *Danger Within*; maniac bomber on an air liner in *Jetstorm*; and a plane crash survivor on an island awaiting an imminent hydrogen bomb test in *S.O.S. Pacific*. Of such stuff the British cinema of the 1950s was made.

'ACTOR–MANAGER'

Attenborough says 'I am really an actor–manager'. During the sixties he was able to realise this position in the cinema, and thereby gain firmer control over his work and career. The co-writer of *The Baby and the Battleship* and *Danger Within* was Bryan Forbes, who also acted alongside Attenborough in the former film. The two struck up a long-lasting friendship which developed into a creative partnership. The seeds were sown when the actor Michael Craig outlined his own hopes of going into production while he, the director Guy Green and Attenborough were sheltering from a sandstorm during the making of *Sea of Sand*.

So it was that Attenborough and Forbes set up their own production company, Beaver Films, and with Guy Green and Michael Craig set about making *The Angry Silence*, based on an idea by Craig and his brother Richard Gregson (who eventually became one of Attenborough's agents). They took the project to British Lion, at that time run by the Boulting Brothers, Frank Launder and Sidney Gilliat. British Lion felt it was uncommercial, but nevertheless offered to finance the film if it could be made for £100,000. Attenborough and Forbes reduced the original budget of £140,000 by persuading various of their collaborators to defer their salaries, as they did themselves. The costumiers Bermans and the film's lawyers and accountants also extended credit and the film was eventually made for £92,000.

Attenborough co-produced *The Angry Silence* with Forbes, and starred, as the workman ostracized by his workmates, thanks to the machinations of sinister and disruptive political forces in the factory. A natural Attenborough subject, the story is about the perils and inhumanity of stupefied, unthinking mob action.

The Angry Silence
(1960). Attenborough
(co-producer) as the
ostracized factory
worker, Tom Curtis

Attenborough had meanwhile also formed, with Forbes, Guy Green, Michael Relph, Basil Dearden and Jack Hawkins, an independent distribution company, Allied Film Makers. He played in the company's highly successful first venture, a comedy thriller, *League of Gentlemen*.

Beaver's second production was *Whistle Down the Wind*, based on a story by Mary Hayley Bell, Mrs John Mills, about a group of children who believe a fugitive murderer to be Christ. This time Attenborough produced and Forbes, encouraged by Attenborough's unequivocal advocacy, directed for the first time.

After a rewarding comic role as a vain Welsh playwright in Sidney Gilliat's *Only Two Can Play*, he co-produced, this time with James Woolf, *The L-Shaped Room*, a portrait of the denizens of a cheap London lodging house, seen through the eyes of a young girl seeking an abortion. Forbes again directed, with Leslie Caron and Tom Bell in the leading roles.

Several acting assignments intervened between this and Beaver's fourth and last production. *All Night Long* was *Othello* updated to a

London jazz club. *The Dock Brief*, adapted from John Mortimer's television entertainment, was a comic *tour-de-force*. Peter Sellers plays the disastrously incompetent barrister; Attenborough his hapless client – a mild seed merchant who freely admits the murder of his exasperating wife. Sellers' brilliant caricature was outclassed by Attenborough's subtly shaded comic performance. In *The Great Escape*, an American production of Paul Brickhill's book, he was back in the air force as a Squadron Leader, expert in the arts of escape. The film marked his first meeting with Steve McQueen.

Beaver's final production, *Seance on a Wet Afternoon*, produced by Attenborough and admirably written and directed by Forbes, was undoubtedly its best. Kim Stanley received an Oscar nomination for Best Actress. Attenborough's performance won him the Best Actor Award of the British Film Academy and also of the San Sebastian Film Festival. He plays the meek asthmatic husband who humours his disturbed wife (Kim Stanley) by helping her kidnap a child. 'Of all the work I've done in the cinema, that particular performance gave me most satisfaction – due in no small measure to playing opposite that remarkable American actress, Kim Stanley, both of us guided by Bryan with wonderful skill and adroitness.'

The Great Escape (1963) – Attenborough with Gordon Jackson and Steve McQueen

An omnibus film, *The Third Secret* did no credit to anyone involved with it, but John Guillermin's *Guns at Batasi* gave him a role, as RSM Lauderdale, which he himself regarded as the best he had had since Pinkie in *Brighton Rock*. The performance won him the British Film Academy Award as Best Actor for the second time. Attenborough plays a veteran army martinet serving in Africa, facing an impending revolution and struggling to understand the new political subtleties of the end of Empire. He was coached for the part (and the vocal power it required) by the legendary and formidable RSM Britten at Chelsea Barracks; and, despite the presence of actors like Flora Robson and Jack Hawkins, his performance single-handedly gives the film integrity and cohesion.

Now deeply committed to the problems of finding finance for *Gandhi*, and using up his personal funds in developing this most cherished project, he needed lucrative work. It was provided by a succession of Hollywood assignments, and for more than a year he worked in California. *The Flight of the Phoenix* (1966), directed by Robert Aldrich, was an adventure drama about the tensions among the crew of a crashed plane, stranded in the Arabian desert. Attenborough played the nerve-shattered navigator, while the pilot was James Stewart. 'The prospect of working with yet another of Hollywood's living legends was a stroke of good fortune given to few people whose home is on the other side of the Atlantic.'[17] Much of the location shooting of *The Sand Pebbles* (1967), directed by Robert Wise, was in Taipei. Attenborough, who won a Golden Globe for his performance, was again teamed with Steve McQueen: a strong mutual admiration and affection grew up between the two actors; and Attenborough feels McQueen's early death as a personal loss.

He was cast almost by chance in Richard Fleischer's *Dr Dolittle*, since he happened to be working at the same studio when it was discovered that the actor originally chosen for the role of Albert Blossom – the showman whose pride and joy is the two-headed llama, the Pushmi-Pullyu – could neither dance nor sing. Attenborough showed that he could – well enough to get a Golden Globe for his short role. Back in Britain he had a rich part as a protean swindler in Basil Dearden's *Only When I Larf*. His

The Flight of the Phoenix (1966) – Richard Attenborough with James Stewart

With Steve McQueen in
The Sand Pebbles (1967)

meeting with the writer Len Deighton was to prove a factor in launching Attenborough's directorial career a year later. Not even Attenborough could save *The Bliss of Mrs Blossom*, a lingerie farce in which he co-starred with Shirley MacLaine.

As the sixties turned to the seventies, many of Attenborough's acting assignments now look as if they were accepted as means to the end which was *Gandhi*: 'I'd spent so much money on trying to make it a reality that there came a point where I could hardly pay the gas bill.' *The Magic Christian* was a sketch film to showcase Ringo Starr. In *The Last Grenade* Attenborough plays a dim military man whose marriage is on the rocks. Laurence Olivier as Mr Creakle and Attenborough, playing the small role of Mr Tungay, steal the show in Delbert Mann's dull, TV-oriented *David Copperfield*.

An adaptation of Joe Orton's *Loot* however gave him a rich comedy role as the obtuse, snooping and sanctimoniously corrupt Truscott of the Yard. It was followed by the role of the psychiatrist in Dick Clements' film of Frederic Raphael's adaptation of Iris Murdoch's *A Severed Head* (1971).

The best of Attenborough's later parts however was as the murderer John Reginald Christie in Richard Fleischer's *10 Rillington Place*, a rare instance of a British commercial film impelled by powerful – indeed

As the murderer John
Reginald Christie in
10 Rillington Place
(1970), with John Hurt
and Judy Geeson

passionate – social motives. 'A Conservative MP was in the process of
introducing a private member's bill to reinstate capital punishment. And
that was the motivating force that drove all of us to get the film, based
on Ludovic Kennedy's masterly account of the case, made and made
quickly. We're not politicians, we're not writers, we're film-makers. And
we wanted to make a statement about the barbarism of the whole business. Here, in the case of Timothy Evans, was a particular example, of a
boy who had done nothing wrong, yet who was hanged for Reginald
Christie's crimes'. Attenborough did not relish the role, but 'felt that
steeping myself in this particular character, however unpleasant, would
be worthwhile if, as a result, people were persuaded that hanging was
not only barbarous but could cause irretrievable miscarriages of
justice.'[18] His performance is all the more sinister and effective for its
touches of macabre comedy.

And Then There Were None (1975), Peter Collinson's version of
Agatha Christie's *Ten Little Indians* (in former days *Ten Little Niggers*) was
'pretty dreadful', Attenborough remembers; 'Nevertheless, the salary that
I received allowed me to pay off my debts, reduce my overdraft to more
reasonable proportions and keep going for a further few months.'[19]

The same perhaps was true of a supporting role as a whiskery Indian
officer in Michael Anderson's *Conduct Unbecoming*; as well as perform-

ances which proved the principal distinction of two latter-day Otto Preminger pictures, *Rosebud* and particularly *The Human Factor*. Two of his last acting performances before the nineties however gave him special satisfaction – for quite different reasons. In Douglas Hickox' *Brannigan* (1975) he played a London policeman to John Wayne's Chicago counterpart. 'I remember *Brannigan* with some amusement because it contained one scene in which ostensibly I laid "Duke" Wayne low with a right-hander to his chin!'

In *The Chess Players*, he worked with the great Bengali director Satyajit Ray, whom he had met at the Delhi Film Festival, during his continuing quest to set up his film biography of *Gandhi*. When Ray asked Attenborough if he would act in one of his films he replied – as he was later to repeat to Steven Spielberg – 'If you offered me the telephone directory to act, I'd do it.'

The film was made in an antiquated studio in Calcutta, and Attenborough marvelled at Ray's ability to make great films in such primitive circumstances. The equipment was outmoded, and with no air conditioning, the doors had to be left open, letting in all the noise from outside – which certainly must have made concentration for the actors somewhat difficult, and particularly for Attenborough, tightly costumed and suffering Calcutta temperatures well over 100 degrees Farenheit. 'None of this seems to faze him,' says Attenborough; 'He was meticulous. I've never known anyone spend so much time in terms of set-ups. He'll be glued to the view-finder for five minutes, and then will go over to a table on the set and move a glass a couple of inches. It's this kind of attention to detail that contributes to the calibre of the work. Even so, progress was not tardy. We completed twenty-six minutes of screen time in ten days. He had no first assistant. He commanded the floor. Nobody else raised a voice'.[20] 'I count working for him as one of the milestones of my acting career.' [21] After Ray's death, Attenborough was to play an active part in the creation of a Foundation, of which he is President, designed to commemorate the work of Ray through helping new film-makers.

OH! WHAT A LOVELY WAR

Attenborough's debut as director was a triumph. Surprisingly, it appears to have been one of the least-planned incidents in a career which has generally been plotted with such care.

'I never had any thought of directing, and I certainly never had any thought of breaking up my immensely happy partnership with Bryan Forbes. I loved acting and I loved producing – I think the contribution of the creative producer is often very underrated. It is true I had for a long time wanted to direct *Gandhi*, but that was really by virtue of the material. I was totally blinkered in my determination to make that movie. So that when *Oh! What A Lovely War* arrived, my reaction was

*Oh! What a Lovely War
– Attenborough on
Brighton Pier*

Diplomatic group from *Oh! What a Lovely War* (1969). Back row, standing: Paul Daneman as Tsar Nicholas II, Kenneth More as Kaiser Wilhelm, John Clements as General von Moltke. Seated: Ralph Richardson as Sir Edward Grey, Ian Holm as President Poincaré, John Gielgud as Count Berchtold

not at all "Ah, here at last is an opportunity to direct a movie", but total amazement that anyone should think of my doing it – and why this particular subject?'

His involvement began in the summer of 1967 when John Mills asked him to read a screen adaptation, on which he had worked with Len Deighton, of the Joan Littlewood stage show. He and Deighton, Mills said, wondered if Attenborough would be interested in directing it?

Oh! What a Lovely War had evolved in a strange fashion. The beginning was a modest one-hour radio feature, *The Long, Long Trail – Soldiers' Songs of the First World War*, devised by Charles Chilton and originally broadcast at Christmas 1961. The programme traced the history of the war and changing attitudes to it, through its songs, and with the help of two narrators – one representing official history, the other the viewpoint of the man in the trenches.

Interest in the First World War had been stimulated by the BBC's multi-part documentary, and Charles Chilton's own television version of his original radio programme. In 1963 Joan Littlewood decided to develop *The Long, Long Trail* into a musical for Theatre Workshop. Chilton collaborated on the script with the Canadian Marxist playwright Ted Allen (co-author of *Double Image,* in which Attenborough acted on stage in 1956), to produce an entertainment in the then modish Brechtian style. In this, the war was presented as a show given by a pierrot company, the Merry Roosters. The stage version of *Oh! What a Lovely War* opened at the Theatre Royal, Stratford East on 19 March 1963, transferred to Wyndhams on 20 June of that year, and ran for a total of more than five hundred performances.

'I had seen the show and adored it. And to this day I don't think the film, because it is derivative, was as important a piece of work as the play. And I don't think its execution was as good as the play, which had such perception and originality of form.'

At first sceptical about filming a show that was of its essence so theatrical, Attenborough was convinced by the devices of the Deighton script. 'I thought and still think that Len's idea of moving the action on to Brighton pier, and creating the circumstance and possibility of moving from fantasy to reality, was a stroke of genius in terms of film adaptation.' Moreover, 'The pacifism that attracted me to *Gandhi* was epitomized in the screenplay. It rang the same bells for me.'[22]

The film script sets the action on Brighton Pier, where the Merry Roosters attract the public with a Guards' band rendering of the song 'Oh! What a Lovely War'. From this point, 'With impressive dexterity, the film shifts between different types of stylisation. The pier stands for the home front, the high command, the detached world of political decision. The generals gather and politicians confer against a luminous white background; upon its main, slowly deteriorating, level, soldiers bid their families farewell, pacifist meetings gather, munition workers chat; above it, on top of a helter-skelter, Haig and the general staff issue their battle orders. The front-line is situated on the Sussex Downs and no attempt is made to disguise the fact; we are never shown any face-to-face combat and indeed the only time the German troops appear is at the "unofficial armistice" of Christmas 1914, when the two sides meet in No Man's Land.'[23] The film adaptation used the pierrot leader – played in the film by Joe Melia – as a protean character to link the scenes.

Attenborough was won to the project, agreed to co-produce it with Brian Duffy and Len Deighton, and set about securing financing. He met Charles Bluhdorn, who had just taken over Paramount. In Bluhdorn's suite at the Dorchester Hotel, Attenborough 'unblushingly' acted, danced and sang most of the script. Bluhdorn was so impressed that he pledged the necessary financial support on condition that Attenborough could guarantee six major stars. Attenborough rashly assured him that this was as good as done.

In fact he managed to bring together the cream of the entire British acting profession. His first approach was to Laurence Olivier who promptly agreed to accept any part, however small, on an Equity minimum daily rate salary. In the event he produced a marvellous cameo performance as Field Marshal Sir John French. Olivier's example helped immeasurably in recruiting other actors of the stature of Ralph Richardson, John Gielgud and Michael Redgrave. For Jack Hawkins, *Oh! What a Lovely War* was his first work since an operation for throat

cancer had left him voiceless. Attenborough created for him the non-speaking but impressive role of Emperor Franz Josef of Austria.

'When I went to Olivier, after having thus lied to Charlie Bluhdorn, it was not merely loyalty and affection that made him agree. He believed passionately that the artist, the performer should not merely be inter-pretative. The RSC after Quayle was essentially a directors' theatre. Olivier always believed that the National Theatre should be run by an actor–manager, and that the performer should provide the artistic drive and conception. He later asked me to join him at the National, with the prospect of becoming his successor – which is why I had to choose between doing *Young Winston* and going to the National.

'In my doing *Oh! What a Lovely War* he recognised the possibility for an actor to take his knowledge and perceptions into creative work. It was because of this in large measure that I was able to acquire the indus-try and theatrical backing for the movie, quite apart from the finance. It was Larry really who said "This is right. Here is an opportunity to extend the concept of the actor–manager in the theatre to actor–manager in the cinema." And I suppose in truth that is what I really am in the way I make my movies – an actor–manager.

'When I first read the script, though, I rang Johnny Mills and asked him, "Why in God's name did you ask me?" He said, "Well, Len and I

thought we either had to find someone who was unbelievably experienced in this sort of subject matter, or someone who knew absolutely
nothing, so might risk things which nobody else would. We decided on
the latter." He was of course teasing me. But I also think my inexperi-
ence was something of an advantage. I tried things which, had I been
more experienced, I might well not have risked. So when the crew said,
"Oh you can't do that. It won't work", I would ask, "Why?" over and
over again; and insisted on trying things that I was told wouldn't work
and had never been done. This was at a time when television had still
not made its full impact on our perception – the speed and juxtaposition
of situations and images which is now totally accepted. So at that time it
had to be someone of naive perception who would use that kind of
cutting from sequence to sequence, between fantasy and reality. It was
not so much daring as naivety, in saying, well, we'll just try it and see
what happens. And, by gosh it worked, I was really able to do it thanks
to the help of three vital people – an unbelievably wonderful first assistant, Claude Watson, who died of cancer not long afterwards; a
phenomenal continuity girl, Ann Skinner, who is now a producer in her
own right; and Don Ashton the production designer who was sadly lost
to the cinema when he became an international interior architectural
designer. Without them and Gerry Turpin and Ronnie Taylor as cinematographer and operator respectively, I would never have made the
movie. They were prepared to accept that I required answers.

'An example of the way we chanced our arms was for instance the
way we cut instantaneously from the high command surveying the battle
front from the top of the Brighton helter-skelter, to their arrival at the
front.

'Then, early in the film, I wanted to make a transition without
dissolves or mixes, moving an actor in one and the same shot from a
shooting range on the end of the pier, where he was dressed in civvies,
to the trenches where he would be in uniform. So I started the shot on
a side view of the civilian, moved the camera round on to the target and
the spectators, and by the time we got back to the soldier, completing a
360 degree turn, he was in the trenches. We achieved this by changing
the final camera angle, so that this time we saw him only against the sky.
And, in the time it had taken the camera to complete its move, two

wardrobe men and a make-up artist had come in and ripped off his clothes and re-dressed him completely.

'The normal way to achieve this effect would have been simply to cut away or dissolve. But, by staying with the shot, we took the audience with us, persuading them unconsciously to swallow the fantasy. They then readily accepted that the style of the film was going to take them seamlessly from fantasy to reality and reality to fantasy.'

Len Deighton left the production after disagreements. In curious consequence the film carries no script credit. 'I never quite understood the reasons for Len leaving the movie. I think it was partially because he was not absolutely in favour of some of the things I wanted to do; but basically I suspect it sprang from disagreements with his erstwhile partner Brian Duffy, the co-producer.'

Oh! What a Lovely War opened in March 1969. Notices were equally enthusiastic on both sides of the Atlantic. The usually laconic American trade paper *Variety* wrote: 'Richard Attenborough's debut as a film director is an occasion that warrants such over-used, but not in this case, showbiz verbal coinage as "fabulous", "sensational", "stupendous", etc. His work also happens to be dedicated, exhilarating, shrewd, mocking, funny, emotional, witty, poignant and technically brilliant.' Among the nearly unanimous London reviewers, one of the most sensitive, Philip French, in *Sight and Sound* concluded, 'What we sense in the film – more clearly than in the radio version or the calculatedly didactic left-wing stage version – is a national meditation, almost in the religious sense, upon the experience of the Great War. There is no rancour and no easy scapegoats. The Littlewood scenes involving the machinations of munition manufacturers have been dropped, and a decent regard for the losses suffered by the "officer-class" (to which there was but a single reference in the play) introduced. The presence of what seems to be the British acting profession in its entirety, with the larger roles going to the lesser known players, strikes one less as a series of self-conscious guest performances than as a participation in a solemn, though far from humourless, act.'

YOUNG WINSTON

A fter *Oh! What a Lovely War*, a career as director was inescapable. Attenborough received a number of propositions, including an invitation from Carl Foreman to direct his script, *Young Winston*, for Foreman's own production company. The project had begun many years before, in 1961, when Winston Churchill had seen and been impressed by Foreman's *Guns of Navarone*. Foreman was consequently summoned by Churchill, who proposed to him a film based on his autobiographical accounts of his adventurous early life. Foreman's interviews with Churchill were evidently not entirely easy. The old gentleman was very deaf, and impatiently expected the film to be ready in three months' time.

Foreman for his part was only gradually won to the idea as he discovered the fascination of Churchill's story. The neglected child of rich parents, shipped off to boarding school at seven, young Winston worshipped his beautiful, American-born mother from afar; and consistently failed to win either the approval or the affection of his father, Lord Randolph Churchill. Less than brilliant at Harrow, he went on to Sandhurst. As an officer in the Hussars he saw service in Cuba, India and the Sudan. In the South African War he was taken prisoner by the Boers, but escaped, to become a national hero. In 1901 he was elected to Parliament.

By 1969 Foreman had reduced these 27 eventful years, and a mass of research, to a manageable screenplay. To cope with the necessary truncations of the narrative, and such tricky themes as Lord Randolph's fatal venereal disease and Lady Churchill's infidelities, he introduced a

Young Winston (1972): Simon Ward

bold structural device: an 'interviewer' who from time to time quizzes the principal characters in the style of the historic interviews conducted by John Freeman in the BBC's 'Face to Face' series.

Foreman considered directing the film himself, but decided the job should go to a British director. He and Attenborough met to discuss the project on New Year's Day 1970, when Foreman additionally proposed that Attenborough should play Lord Randolph Churchill. Attenborough declined to act and direct at the same time, 'feeling that the preoccupations of each responsibility would damage the execution of the other'. He cast Robert Shaw in the role.

'Carl was massively complimentary about *Oh! What a Lovely War.* When he asked me to read his script for *Young Winston* I was enormously intrigued by it. And of course it was a marvellous thing to do because for my generation, whatever you thought of Churchill politically, he was a goddamned hero. I genuinely did, and do believe he saved Europe and thereby saved Western civilization as we have become accustomed to it. It would have re-emerged, no doubt, the same way that it has in Russia. But I believe that without question he stood alone.

'I was however apprehensive, because Carl was not only the producer, making the film for his own company, but he was the writer too. So to suggest that the director could have any sort of autonomy was nonsense. I had tasted blood a little on *Oh! What a Lovely War*, in that although I produced jointly with Brian Duffy, and although the film was made for Paramount, I really did have total control. So I was very doubtful about accepting this new situation.

'At the same time I was being courted by Laurence Olivier, who wanted me to play both Sky Masterson in *Guys and Dolls* and Shylock at the National Theatre. He also had the idea of my joining him as an associate, with the prospect of succeeding him as director. This was all part of his absolute conviction that the National should be actor–manager-led. I was pushed towards the National by the knowledge that I would have no right of final say on *Young Winston*. But in the end I felt I was not intellectually up to the National job and in any case I was perhaps even by that time too much in love with the cinema. I knew that if I had gone to the National for seven or ten years, it would have been goodbye to movies. So I decided on *Young Winston*.

'I never really fully agreed with the script, and I think that is where we went wrong. Carl would let me have certain emendations to the screenplay; but it was agreed between us that in such cases I would shoot two versions – what I thought would work and what Carl thought would work. This applied particularly to the device of the 'interviewers' which was Carl's invention: the actual manner of its presentation was mine, but the concept was his.

'I did win my first and most vital battle however, which was the choice of Simon Ward to play Churchill. Carl had another candidate, but he eventually allowed me to have my way. And I am immensely happy because that was a really remarkable performance. I had another victory in the casting of Anne Bancroft as Jennie Jerome, Churchill's mother.' The supporting cast was full of favourite Attenborough actors, including John Mills, Jack Hawkins, Ian Holm, Anthony Hopkins and Gerald Sim,

With Simon Ward (centre) on the set of Young Winston (1972)

Attenborough's brother-in-law, a charming and reliable supporting player who appears like a mascot in most of his films up to and including *Shadowlands*. Foreman himself, in interviews after the event, cheerfully suggested that all the casting choices were unanimous.

'So we started shooting, and it is no good pretending that everything about it was hunky-dory. I had enormous respect for Carl and no small affection, but he operated in a different way from me. And the further we got into the production, the greater were my concerns about the script.

'Finally, when I had cut the movie, and cut it as I felt it ought to be, Carl re-cut the film in a number of areas. He had a perfect right to do so. He was producer and screenwriter – I was engaged as a working director.

'There was never any open animosity in terms of decisions as to how we should conduct ourselves with the unit. We didn't come to blows in any sense. He behaved perfectly properly, and as I say, he was totally within his rights. He made it clear from the word go that it was his idea, he had raised the money, he had the contract with Columbia, he was the producer, he was the writer, he had obtained the rights from Churchill. I was the director.

'But in a number of areas it is not the movie that I would have made. He didn't like the close camerawork that I chose. He wanted it more in medium shot, less penetrative, I felt. And so it distressed me in a number of instances when I saw the finished film.

'This is the only film where I have not had creative autonomy as director. Joe Levine gave me my head entirely on *A Bridge Too Far* and *Magic*. On *Gandhi* there was no other person involved. And after the success of *Gandhi* Marti Baum, my agent, was able to insist on my right of final cut. The company that financed *A Chorus Line* was represented by the duo of Jerry Parencio and Norman Lear. They hated the movie when I had finished it anyway!'

During the production of *Young Winston* Attenborough called the film 'an intimate epic – an epic subject which is the frame for, and the setting for, an intimate story, which is really three stories – those of Winston, his father Randolph and his mother Jennie'.

The concern for historical veracity and opulent staging that were to

Young Winston: charge against the Boers in South Africa

characterise Attenborough's later biographical films were already evident in *Young Winston*. Foreman recalled that at their first meeting, 'although he had read the script and was excited by it, he wanted to know my sources. I told him and by the time we met again, he had not only checked them out but had uncovered additional research himself.'[24]

Filming took six months. The South African scenes were shot in South Wales, and India and the Sudan in Morocco. English locations included Blenheim Palace, Harrow, and Windsor race track. Sets at Shepperton studios included a massive recreation of the House of Commons as it looked in 1901.

The film opened in the summer of 1972 and despite Attenborough's continuing misgivings, it was generally received with enthusiasm, even attracting favourable comparison with *Lawrence of Arabia* of recent reverent memory. Unaware of the tensions involved in the script, and Attenborough's dislike of working without autonomy, John Russell Taylor wrote in *The Times*, 'Controlling it all, the sober but sensitive directorial hand of Richard Attenborough … There is nothing here quite to match the imaginative and emotional lift of the best moments in *Oh! What a Lovely War* but nothing either to contradict our first opinion of Mr Attenborough's considerable talents as a director as well as an actor.'

A BRIDGE TOO FAR

A *Bridge Too Far* – a military epic based on Cornelius Ryan's account of General Montgomery's attempt to establish a bridgehead behind German lines in 1942, 'Operation Market Garden' – was again not Attenborough's personal choice of project. No doubt its possibilities for an anti-war statement appealed to him, but many other war stories could have served the purpose as well or better.

The film was, in fact, the unlikely pet project of the colourful Joe Levine. Levine, then approaching 70, was perhaps the last of the mythical rag-trade-to-riches movie moguls. Born and raised in the slums of Boston, he was the youngest of six children of an immigrant tailor who died when Joseph Edward was four. From infancy he had to work to contribute to the support of the family. At fourteen he left school to be errand boy in a dress factory. He rose to salesman and by twenty had his own dress shop. After various other enterprises he discovered the cinema and took over an art house, the Lincoln Theatre in New Haven. His opening film was *Un Carnet de Bal*, which showed him that there could be money in art movies. Moving on to distribution, he brought to America some of the great European films of the forties and fifties, notably the Italian neo-realists and early Fellini. His most celebrated enterprise however was the selling of *Hercules* in 1959. Levine himself had no illusions about this shabby sandal epic which every other distributor had declined to take on. He doctored the film a little, and launched it with an aggressive sales campaign, using television advertising for a film for the first time, and released it with 600 prints – at that time an unprecedented figure. *Hercules* grossed twenty million dollars, and helped launch Levine's success in the sixties as an independent producer, with films like *The Graduate*.

In 1974 Levine discovered Cornelius Ryan's *A Bridge Too Far,* and determined to make the biggest war movie in history. He shrewdly recognised his ideal director in Attenborough. For his part, Attenborough was partly lured by Levine's declared enthusiasm eventually to produce his most cherished project, *Gandhi* – after *A Bridge Too Far*.

Attenborough's view of Levine was to be soured by later unhappy experiences involving *Gandhi*, though in longer retrospect his memories are warmer: 'I owe Joe a lot. I recall he saw *Oh! What a Lovely War* and went barmy about it. I remember him walking from the Warwick preview theatre in Audley Square to the Dorchester, crying all the way – which is why *A Bridge Too Far* came about, I'm sure.

'I thought it was unscriptable. I could not fathom how something so complex could be given dramatic shape. If you are dealing with fiction you are free to do what you want. But when you are dealing with docu-drama there are certain honour-bound criteria from which you simply cannot depart.

'However, in New York Joe sent me to meet a writer. This was William Goldman. At that time his inhibition and shyness made him almost mono-syllabic; and I left him certain that it would not work. However by the time I got back to Joe's office he had called to say he wanted to work with me.' Goldman's recollection of the same meeting is that it was pleasant, 'except that afterward, his impression was that I didn't want to do the movie and mine was that he definitely didn't want me to do it'.[25] The misunderstanding overcome, 'we became very close. I have probably worked with him closer than with any other writer – apart of course for Bryan Forbes in the days of our partnership. Bill is an eminently practical, precise man. I can see his office now, with the various incidents that went to make up Operation Market Garden stuck on a wall. So you could see at a glance the whole of the Polish or the Dutch campaign. Bill would take pages off the wall, and place them on the table as he decided on the order of scenes. I think it was a staggeringly successful treatment of an almost impossible subject. I thought him wonderful, and still do – his ability to put into nine words fifteen different pieces of observation or factual contribution is unique. He is quite extraordinary. His management of the various story-lines was utterly brilliant. I think very few critics recognised the scale of his achievement in organising the vast spread of incidents.'

Goldman's previous scripts had included *Butch Cassidy and the Sundance Kid* and *All the President's Men*, and he was already a legend for his structural skills. Embarking on the script he found that apart from the 650 closely-printed pages of Ryan's book there was a vast literature on Arnhem – 'the British cherish their disasters.'[26]

Dramatically the story presented huge problems. The logistics of the operation were in themselves hard to explain. Montgomery had intended Operation Market Garden to put a quick end to the war, by Christmas 1944. His plan was to air-lift 35,000 Allied paratroops, mainly American, three hundred miles and drop them behind German lines in Holland. While they seized and held a series of vital bridges, a British armoured corps of 30,000 was to break through German lines, cross the bridges and then make a dash over the last and most crucial, at Arnhem, directly into the industrial heart of Germany.

The plan failed, which was a fairly substantial handicap in dramatic terms. Yet it was hard to turn it into tragedy, in the formal sense, since all the principal characters in the story survived. Also there were too many individual stories to choose from: Arnhem earned no less than five V.C.s. Eventually Goldman found his clue: 'I realised, for all its size and complexity, *Bridge* was a cavalry-to-the-rescue story – one in which the cavalry fails to arrive, ending, sadly, one mile short.'[27]

Working on his firm principal that a film must always enter a story at the latest possible point, Goldman began with the parachute landing near Arnhem of the First Airborne Division under Lieutenant-Colonel Frost, who was historically the principal commander and hero of the action. They find themselves surrounded by two German divisions which they had expected, on the contrary, to be in full retreat.

Meanwhile the US Airborne Division under Major General Taylor takes Eindhoven and joins up with a ground column of the British XX Corps under Lieutenant Colonel Vandeleur. Their object of consolidating the bridgeheads is frustrated by the destruction of the Son Bridge.

Meanwhile, giving up hope of expected reinforcements, Brigadier-General Gavin of the US 82nd Airborne Division risks a daylight attack across the Rhine, which succeeds, thanks largely to German miscalculations. The 82nd however delays a further advance on Arnhem, waiting for the arrival of the main British and American forces.

The isolated paratroopers who have held one end of the Arnhem bridge for four days are finally forced to surrender: the rest of their forces have lost communication, and the much-needed supplies have been dropped behind German positions.

After delays from bad weather, the Polish Parachute Brigade under Major-General Sosabowski finally intervenes, only to be practically wiped out while attempting a night assault on Elst.

The battle having lasted nine days without achieving the intended breakthrough to Arnhem, Lieutenant Colonel Brian Horrocks halts the operation. The force withdraws across the Rhine.

Montgomery pronounces the battle almost entirely successful; but Lieutenant-Colonel Browning, who co-ordinated it from England, reflects that the attempt seriously over-reached itself.

To relate this complex, multiple action was a tall order for the film makers; and the overall clarity of the action is tribute to Goldman and Attenborough. The achievement is even more remarkable considering that – unusually for a production on this scale and uncomfortably for Attenborough – Goldman's script was still not completed when the film went into principal pre-production. This was the consequence of the very tight production schedule imposed by Levine's apparently whimsical determination that the premiere should be on 15 June 1977 – a date which appeared to have no historical significance of any kind. For the right weather conditions, the six-month shooting period had to be precisely planned from April to October 1976; and the film's schedule was constructed to fit these dates.

Levine's strategy for pre-selling the film depended on recruiting an all-star cast. From Britain Attenborough was able to recruit for him Laurence Olivier, Anthony Hopkins, Dirk Bogarde, Sean Connery and Michael Caine. The American cast was led by Robert Redford, James Caan, Gene Hackman, Ryan O'Neal and Elliott Gould. The exorbitant demands of his agents made it impossible to include in the cast Steve McQueen, at that time the top box-office star alongside Redford – 'though I know if I could have reached him personally at that moment he would have made it possible'. The all-star cast in no way dismayed Attenborough, who not only hugely

With Robert Redford on the set of *A Bridge Too Far* (1977)

Michael Caine in
A Bridge Too Far

enjoyed working with such distinguished peers, but felt that faces so
readily recognisable were vital in helping audiences keep track of such a
large number of characters.

The cinematographer was the incomparable Geoffrey Unsworth, a
long-standing and close friend of Attenborough, who regards him as 'one
of the greatest lighting cameramen the cinema has known'. The crew also
included Terence Marsh as production designer. The principal art director was Stuart Craig who was to figure importantly on most of
Attenborough's later films. Inevitably the first assistant was the formidable David Tomblin, with his proven reputation for handling mass scenes.'
'By the time shooting began', Attenborough recalled, 'we were so well
equipped we could have fought Russia – and won.' Attenborough was
particularly concerned that the actors should look and move like soldiers.
Before production a group of thirty or more actors were posted to a
specially created training camp in Holland, for a fortnight's drill under
the instruction of two R.S.M.s. They were known to the crew as the
A.P.A.s – Attenborough's Private Army. 'They were the "foot-soldiers" of
the cast, and had a vital role in the interests of professionalism and
tempo.'

The scale of the production brought many hazards, but the weather,
which was crucial, remained favourable. Goldman recalls in his book
Adventures in the Screen Trade the 'Million-Dollar Hour' that came at the

Inspecting 'Attenborough's Private Army'

end of shooting. The Nijmegen Bridge, a vital location, was one of the busiest routes in Holland; and the authorities were only prepared to close it for one hour on each of three Sunday mornings. The last of these was also Robert Redford's last contracted day. The scene was huge, and if anything had prevented its completion within the allotted hour, the costs of Redford's overages and of keeping on the crew and the rest of the cast and extras would have added an instant million dollars to the budget. As it was, the weather was favourable and the scene was shot in time. *A Bridge Too Far* was brought in under schedule and in time for Levine's 15 July 1977 opening.

Levine's pre-selling had been so energetic that the film was four million dollars in profit before it was ever seen. Levine had made a point of showing the work in progress to innumerable potential buyers; and the unmixed enthusiasm at these previews had enormously encouraged the entire unit. They were unprepared therefore for a very mixed critical reception, particularly in America. Goldman recalls that they were especially irked by disbelief of details in a film which, like all Attenborough's historical and biographical undertakings, was meticulously true to fact. In particular reviewers complained that Ryan O'Neal appeared too young. In fact the character he played, General James Gavin, was at the time exactly the same age as the actor, and indeed famous as the youngest general in the American Army. 'I've never been involved in a

A Bridge Too Far: at
Arnhem – the bridge
that was too far

project where authenticity was more sought after and achieved. And in
the end, as far as many American critics were concerned, that may have
proved our undoing.'[28] Representative of the criticisms levelled against
the film in Britain was John Pym's comments in the *Monthly Film
Bulletin* – never Attenborough's most sympathetic audience. After
complaining about the fragmented narrative, the top-heavy list of stars
and the lack of the kind of focal point provided by Jack Hawkins'
Allenby in *Lawrence of Arabia*, Pym concludes: 'the enterprise as a
protracted whole is so wearily, expensively predictable that by the end
the viewer will in all likelihood be too enervated to note Attenborough's
prosaic moral epilogue. Liv Ullman's family make their way along the
horizon, pulling their belongings in a cart: a small boy marches behind
with a toy rifle on his shoulder.' Other critics were more responsive to
this characteristic irony; and there was certainly a large enough body of
critical supporters to save Attenborough and Goldman from paranoia.
Philip French wrote in *The Times* that *A Bridge Too Far* was 'among the
best recreated movie combat footage I have ever seen'.

MAGIC

'ㅇne of the joys in working with William Goldman on *A Bridge Too Far* was that we both reached a point of intense admiration for Tony Hopkins' work. He had played Lloyd George in *Young Winston*, which was only his third film role. I persuaded Joe Levine to let me cast him as Lieutenant-Colonel Frost in *A Bridge Too Far*, and we were thrilled by what he did there, too. Bill had a novel which he wanted to adapt, and believed that Tony would be absolutely wonderful for the main role. I read the novel – *Magic* – and absolutely agreed with him. So we went ahead and set up the film with Joe. It cost very little: salaries were negligible.'

Attenborough's fourth film as director was a surprising interlude in a directing career that seemed to be dedicated to handling epic themes, huge and starry casts and big budgets. 'People were surprised, only because there is this expectation about what I do. People expect large epic biographical movies, expensive and I fear on occasion overlong. The expectation is not unreasonable, I suppose. But these films are what they are merely because that is the treatment the subject matter demands. It is always the subject that I enjoy; and in fact *Magic* is the proof of that. What I really love doing is creating circumstances which permit an examination or at least an illustration of human beings under particular circumstances and in particular relationships. And though *Magic* may at first seem to fall outside my genre, it is actually typical of it. It is about three people (or perhaps four if you include the dummy "Fats") – a game of creating characters and interweaving them and allowing them to react on each other. I love working with the actors more than anything else. My technique of directing is always to serve the actors.'

Magic is a melodramatic suspense thriller, with a tight story-line,
concentrated atmosphere and an essential cast of only three people.
Anthony Hopkins plays Corky, a ventriloquist who has overcome early
failure and insecurity by creating a dominant alter ego, in the form of his
mean and foul-mouthed dummy 'Fats'. When asked to take a medical
examination before doing a big television special, Corky flees with Fats
to the Catskills. There he meets Peggy Ann (Ann-Margret), whom he
had admired hopelessly in school-days and who now shows interest in
him, partly because of his success and partly because of boredom with
her husband Duke. Corky is now quite unbalanced and under the influence of Fats, who makes him kill first his agent who comes in search of
him, and then Duke. Finally the jealous Fats, hysterical with fear at the
thought that Corky may leave him, orders Corky to kill Peggy Ann.
Instead he plunges the knife into his own body.

Concentrating his screenplay mainly upon the scenes in the Catskills,
William Goldman was obliged to jettison significant elements of his original novel – the tricky device of a first-person narrative which we
eventually discover is Fats himself; the development of Corky's magical
talent under the guidance of Merlin, one of the book's most interesting
characters, who barely survives in the film. Simplified like this, the script
ran the risk of comparison with previous stories of ventriloquists taken
over by their creations – James Cruze's *The Great Gabbo*, Tod

Anthony Hopkins and
'Fats' in *Magic*

Browning's *Devil Doll* and its 1964 British namesake, and Cavalcanti's
Dead of Night episode, with Michael Redgrave.

Attenborough applied himself to preparing the film as conscientiously
as for his big productions. He and Goldman worked together on the
script for seven months. 'I never take salary until I'm certain that the
screenplay is right', Attenborough has said, 'because then you can walk
away if you want to, saying, "I haven't wasted your money."'[29] He consid-
ers that the tension of a thriller has to be built up in the shooting; 'if you
try to build tension with the scissors alone, you're monkeying around with
the veracity of the actor.'[30] For *Magic* he carefully story-boarded every
set-up, though these drawings were only for his private use.

'I had the sets built early so that I could spend some time in them. At the cabin in the Catskills where Corky goes into retreat, there are two rooms separated by a narrow corridor, which gave me marvellous opportunities to place Corky and Fats apart from one another. Fats could be a little figure at the end of the corridor. And when Fats is virtually "speaking to" Corky, for realism he must do so without any mouth movement if he is at a distance from the ventriloquist's controlling hand, yet if you were to cut close to the dummy with his lips not moving, audience attention would have been dissipated. The camera was always able to move past him quickly, of course, not quite including his lips in frame. But the distancing and separation allowed by that corridor were especially useful.

'Of course, when you go in for so much advance planning, you're in an agony in case it's going to appear self-conscious and pedantic in the result. Also vitally important from the outset is the casting – a usually largely underestimated part of the director's armoury. If you get the casting wrong, you might as well pack up.'[31]

In Anthony Hopkins he had, he said, 'one of the actors – along with Larry in *Richard III* and Brando or Orson Welles in almost anything – who are capable of pushing to the cliff edge of the emotionally bizarre, and yet at the same time remain credible. The role in *Magic* is phenomenally daunting. The actor has to cope with a degree of histrionics, a display of emotional pyrotechnics, such as is rarely called upon. Additionally he has to be able to cope with the technicalities of ventriloquising and operating the dummy, while at the same time displaying this intensity of emotion. As an acting assignment it's probably as difficult as anything one can recall in the cinema.'[32] Hopkins began to practise his magic and ventriloquial skills while still working on his previous role in *International Velvet*. According to Attenborough, Hopkins had Fats sleep alongside him at night, and the dummy was treated with particular respect on the set. On one occasion Fats shouted 'Cut!' when Hopkins had fluffed a scene. 'We all laughed – thought it was terribly witty on Tony's part. But Tony was totally unaware he'd done it.'[33]

Ann-Margret was at first very apprehensive about accepting the role, and required a degree of Attenborough's persuasiveness. She was required to drop her normally highly glamourised image. 'It took courage for her to do it, because of her established persona, the glamour-puss, the sophisticated dolled-up girl; all that armour-plating – eyelashes, eye shadow, brassière, silk stockings, high heels and hair-dos and of course in her cabaret performances, orchestras. These are all part of the exterior image which gives her the courage that actors and actresses need in order to perform.

Anthony Hopkins and Ann-Margret in *Magic*

'So I wasn't just asking her to deglamourise herself, but to abandon all her protective skins. And to say to a girl who a few years ago had that terrible accident and smashed her face very badly (although surgery has virtually removed all sign of it), "Scrub your face, appear on the screen for the first time with no make-up at all, with your hair done up in a little woollen cap, with great outsize woolly sweaters and gumboots," was asking something that must have been very difficult.'[34]

'I adored making *Magic*. I was deeply disappointed in the reception though. It happened with *Chorus Line* too. There were qualities in both movies I thought were really worthy of praise, but which received virtually no recognition, for reasons quite beyond the film as such. Critics objected to the fact that they thought Bill was a poacher – they insisted on making those comparisons with *Dead of Night*. Their objection to *A Chorus Line* was that this foreigner should come in and tamper with an icon of Broadway Americana. The consequence was that actors who made the principal contribution to both films never achieved the recognition or the major credit to which they were entitled.'

Attenborough perhaps underrated the contemporary reviews for *Magic*. Although its reputation has grown, as a cult thriller, on its first appearance it already had enthusiastic critical supporters. Gordon Gow wrote in *Films and Filming*, 'Richard Attenborough directs *Magic* flawlessly, timing its shrewd narrative developments in a superbly knowing way, and inclining us more and more to reach out metaphorically to the hapless Corky as he struggles so deplorably, and yet in a sense so bravely, with his ugly little portion of fate.' Few however rose to the laudatory heights of the American critic, Richard Grenier, writing in *Cosmopolitan*: '*Magic* is an eerie but brilliantly effective psychological thriller that, to my taste, beats any film made by the alleged master of the genre, Alfred Hitchcock.'

GANDHI

---

*G*andhi is the central event of Attenborough's life, not just of his career and creation. He devoted twenty years to the project and risked everything he possessed. Somehow both he and his grand idea survived the years of disappointments, delay, frustration, ridicule and obstruction without becoming stale or sour. By persistence and stubbornness which would have seemed quixotic folly in anyone else, Attenborough finally achieved his ambition – and more. No film made in Britain has ever won greater critical acclaim and commercial success. Its eight Academy Awards – a record till then surpassed only by *Ben Hur* – were only the first of the honours heaped upon the film and its maker. Attenborough's greatest reward though was the certainty that some at least of his audience felt themselves enriched by the encounter with Gandhi, through his screen portrait. That, after all, was what he had most wanted to accomplish.

David Hughes wrote in the *Sunday Times*: 'Its arrival on the screen is a masterly piece of timing. In range of content, nobility of purpose and generosity of spirit Sir Richard Attenborough's achievement coincides with a national longing for just the kind of heart's ease he dispenses. The film is inspired because it offers inspiration … Sir Richard is often heckled for his lack of individual style as a director. He can rest easy. Here with love, with truth, he serves Gandhi well by giving an immensely personal account of him, but on a political scale that travels far beyond the borders of India into the heart of our lives at home.' Perhaps the most remarkable feat of the film was for a Western artist to perceive in Gandhi the essence that was universal. Much that is most significant for the East in Gandhi's teaching is manifested in

Gandhi (1982): Ben
Kingsley as the Mahatma
at the end of the
triumphant Salt March

spiritual qualities elusive to the West. Without betraying or perverting
this aspect of him, Attenborough managed to create an image that
touched the civilizations of East and West alike. An Englishman,
marvelled Gandhi's grandson, 'has enabled the dead Mahatma to speak
to the whole world'.[35]

'The truth is that I don't really want to be a director at all. I just want
to direct that film,' Attenborough said, early in the saga of *Gandhi*.

Films about Gandhi had been mooted in the past by Gabriel Pascal,

Otto Preminger and Michael Powell among others. The idea was first proposed to Attenborough in 1962 by Motilal Kothari, a dedicated follower of Gandhi who had taken upon himself the mission of getting a film made that would teach people about the Mahatma's life and work. He persuaded Attenborough to read Louis Fischer's monumental biography. Attenborough was captivated, though the phrase that seized him and continued foremost in his thinking, was a comment made by Gandhi after suffering a racial insult in South Africa, as a very young man: 'It has always been a mystery to me how men can feel themselves honoured by the humiliation of their fellow beings.'

Attenborough received only discouragement from his friends and associates. His old partner Bryan Forbes declined to attempt a script, because he felt it was impossible to encompass Gandhi's life in a film. Attenborough's agent and lawyer both sensibly felt that the project was far too ambitious for a first-time director – this was seven years before his directing debut with *Oh! What a Lovely War*. His only support came from the dogged Kothari and from Sheila Attenborough, who 'said that if this was something I really desperately cared about and was a story I was determined to tell, then I shouldn't let anything or anybody put me off'.

The approval, good will and collaboration of the Indians was an indispensable first requirement; and Attenborough asked Lord Louis Mountbatten to seek Pandit Nehru's provisional approval for the project. (Attenborough had first met Earl Mountbatten – the last Viceroy and first Governor-General of India – when working on *In Which We Serve*). Thanks to his intercession, Nehru received Attenborough in May and again in November 1962, discussed the project at length, and eventually made it the responsibility of his daughter Indira Gandhi, who with imperturbable energy combated the apathy of legions of Indian civil servants. Nehru gave his opinion that Gandhi was too great a man to be deified; and that he should be played by an English classical actor. His reasoning was that it was essential to have an actor of sufficient experience to sustain the scale of the part, as well as the problems of an age range from seventeen to seventy-nine. His preference was for Alec Guinness. With whirlwind energy, Attenborough spent these brief visits to India – his first ever – meeting every possible surviving associate of Gandhi.

He commissioned a scriptwriter, the Irish novelist Gerald Hanley. At this time he too was convinced that the only possible actor for the role of Gandhi was Alec Guinness; but Guinness was far from willing, believing that the part was an impossible task for an Englishman.

Financial backers were unenthusiastic. The widely feared John Davis of the Rank Organisation was unqualified in his discouragement, yet with an altruism not at all consistent with the popular image of him, he gave Attenborough £5,000 for development. The sum would be returnable if the film were made by another company (Rank were clearly not going to make it), but in other circumstances would be forgotten. 'You have made a number of pictures for us', Davis told him; 'and you are very much part of the British film industry. It would, therefore, in my opinion, be pretty shabby if the Rank Organisation were not to give you a chance to explore this idea to which you seem to be so insanely committed.'[36] Further facilities were made available by the Maharajah of Baroda. During all this period of excited preparation and research, Attenborough was working with Bryan Forbes, both as producer and star of *Seance on a Wet Afternoon*.

In 1963 the *Gandhi* project was shadowed by the death of Pandit Nehru; but later in the year Attenborough met Joseph Levine, who displayed unrestrained enthusiasm for the film. Negotiations were begun with Paramount, with which Levine had a major production deal, and a triumphant press conference was held on 15 December 1963 to announce that shooting would begin on 2 October 1965, the 96th anniversary of Gandhi's birth. 'Needless to say, no actual cash was forthcoming.'

The prospective budget had by this time risen to £5m, but the two most vital ingredients – script and star – were still missing. Hanley's script had turned out extremely long, and failed to capture the vital sense of drama. A succession of writers – Bryan Forbes, approached again, Frederic Raphael, Peter Schaffer and Robert Bolt – declined to take on the project. Donald Ogden Stewart was tried, but his script, *The Day Gandhi Died*, did not chime with Attenborough's ideas. Alec Guinness definitively rejected all persuasion to play the leading role; and Dirk Bogarde, Peter Finch, Albert Finney and Tom Courtenay in turn thought better of it. At this stage Joseph Levine and Embassy Pictures suspended the production. Attenborough worked on at his acting career, using a long Hollywood stint – in *The Flight of the Phoenix, The Sand Pebbles* and *Dr Dolittle* – to make personal approaches to the major distributors, in quest of new financing, totally without success.

Meanwhile Mr Kothari, already a sick man, was growing desperate at the delay. He secured an agreement from Bolt to write the script as long as he could have director approval – which clearly would not include the debutant Attenborough. The ultimate proof of the sincerity of Attenborough's commitment was his willingness, although devastated by the thought, to step down, if that made the realisation of the project more likely.

For a time Fred Zinnemann seemed a likely director; then David Lean (who had been approached by Kothari even before Attenborough). Lean however said he was determined to make a 'little film' first. This turned out to be *Ryan's Daughter* which took him three years to complete.

On 15 January 1970 Motilal Kothari died – on the same day as Gandhi's biographer Louis Fischer. Attenborough had by this time become a director and was working on his second film, *Young Winston*. Between times he had given one of his finest screen performances in *10 Rillington Place*. When he was finishing *Young Winston*, Robert Bolt declared that he would accept Attenborough as a director for his script. Attenborough went back to Joseph Levine, who professed renewed interest, but persuaded Attenborough to make *A Bridge Too Far* in the interim. 'I agreed ultimately, again on the very firm promise volunteered by Joe that on its completion we really would shoot *Gandhi*.' In earnest of his sincerity, Levine reacquired the rights in the project from Paramount, for a sum believed to be $100,000. At this point Anthony Hopkins was the main contender for the leading role.

Ultimately Levine, after years of on-again, off-again, finally pulled out of the project, offering as one of his reasons the difficulty of a Jewish producer collaborating with India, which supported the Arabs in the Middle East. When Attenborough eventually believed he had a way of raising the greater part of the required budget, Levine demanded from Attenborough $2m plus two and a half per cent of the distributor's gross, in exchange for the rights which he had bought for $100,000.

In 1978 Robert Bolt had become seriously ill and unable to work.

Attenborough had to find another writer. He had been impressed by John Briley's script for *Pope Joan*, of which in the initial stages he was the intended director. He invited Briley to write a script; and Briley responded that he wished to initiate an entirely new scenario. This was to be the script of the ultimate film. Concise and firmly structured, within the limits of an episodic biography, Briley's script opens with the assassination and state funeral of Gandhi in 1948, which had always been Attenborough's conception of the film; then flashes back to South Africa in 1893, where Gandhi is a young lawyer, organising non-violent protest against racial discrimination. In 1915, back in India he campaigns for the restoration of a self-sufficient society and non-Western community life, and organises a strike of underpaid mill-workers. This results in violence, the death of British soldiers and the retaliatory massacre at Amritsar, which ends the first part of the film.

Attenborough on the set of *Gandhi* directs a dolly shot with Ben Kingsley and Indian extras

The second part begins with Gandhi's campaign against importation of foreign cloth, as a protest against the Jallinwala Bagh slaughter and

With Ben Kingsley on the set of *Gandhi*

his subsequent jail sentence. This is followed by his march to the sea to make salt illegally, in protest against the Imperial government salt monopoly. In 1931 Gandhi attends the inconclusive All-India conference in London. His mass disobedience campaign in 1942 ends in violence and his own further imprisonment. He is released in 1944, but the independence offered to India is delayed till 1947. There are clashes between India and the newly created Muslim state of Pakistan. Gandhi, now in his late seventies, resolves to fast until the fighting stops. On 31 January 1948 he is shot at a prayer meeting at Birla House, New Delhi. The film closes with the scattering of his ashes in the sacred River Ganges.

After so many years of struggle, when the finance to make *Gandhi* finally materialised, it happened with a speed that seems almost to have taken Attenborough by surprise. The financing was finally assembled by the Canadian Jake Eberts of Goldcrest Films International, without whom, Attenborough readily states, the film would never have been made. Thanks to the support of Mrs Gandhi, who was now Prime Minister, the National Film Development Corporation of India also invested substantially.

Attenborough set about assembling his unit, whose members either were, or would become, his regular collaborators – notably his production collaborator Terence Clegg, his first assistant, David Tomblin with his unique talent for marshalling crowds (the extras for Gandhi's funeral were estimated at 400,000); and the brilliant and resourceful production designer Stuart Craig. The first director of photography was Billy Williams – a slipped disc latterly obliged his replacement by Ronnie Taylor – and the editor John Bloom. The great Indian musician Ravi Shankar composed the music, together with a then little known young English composer, George Fenton. Diana Hawkins, who was to play an increasingly important role as a production executive on all Attenborough's subsequent films, organised the mammoth task of press and publicity.

Over the years two generations of actors – some very improbably – had been considered for the role of Gandhi, in addition to those already approached by Attenborough. They included Peter Finch, Robert de Niro, and Dustin Hoffman. The favourite of one studio was Richard Burton: his presence alone it seems would have ensured financing. The final choice was between John Hurt and Ben Kingsley, who had first been drawn to the attention of Attenborough by his theatre director son Michael Attenborough. Previous screen tests had shown the problems of making an Englishman look convincing as an Indian. Kingsley, whose father was in fact Indian, was finally chosen, and applied himself with extraordinary diligence to the role, shedding weight, taking up yoga, learning to spin cotton, and indeed trying to live life as Gandhi lived, so far as was possible. The huge cast included such distinguished names as John Gielgud, Michael Hordern, John Clements, Trevor Howard and John Mills – few actors refuse even a walk-on part for Attenborough. From younger generations were Ian Charleson, Edward Fox, Martin Sheen and Ian Bannen. Daniel Day Lewis had a line as a South Africn roughneck. Long before, when they were acting together on *The Sand Pebbles*, Attenborough and Candice Bergen had mutually agreed that she should play Margaret Bourke-White: 'with her own parallel experience as a photographer it seemed appropriate to cast her in the role of a world-famous photographer: She knew how to handle the camera.'

Shooting began – miraculously, it must have seemed after the years of struggle – on 26 November 1980. The first scene was filmed at a stone works near Delhi, standing in for Victorian South Africa. Other locations included the garden of Pandit Nehru's house, the former Viceregal palace in New Delhi, now the Presidential residence, Gandhi's birthplace at Porbandar, the Aga Khan Palace at Pune, Bombay, and the gardens of Birla House, where Gandhi was murdered. The extraordinary scene of the funeral was shot on the Rajpath, using eleven camera crews, on the anniversary of the actual event.

The unit left India on 18 April 1981, after 121 days' work. Filming on locations in England continued until Sunday 10 May 1981. One location for which permission to shoot was refused was the door of No. 10 Downing Street. Post-production took up most of the next year; and the film was finally ready for release at the end of 1982 – in time to qualify for the all-important Academy Awards. The film was eventually released world-wide by Columbia Pictures. It had cost some $22m. One third as much again would eventually be spent on distribution and promotion. Both a critical and a popular success, Gandhi was easily to recoup what was for the early eighties a very sizeable investment.

Attenborough had, against all the odds, realised his dream, and consolidated his place in film history.

A CHORUS LINE

Attenborough's American agent, Marti Baum, proposed *A Chorus Line* as his next subject. He felt, said Attenborough, 'that I had an eye and an ear for musical' (as his performance in *Dr Dolittle*, certainly, had indicated). More important, Baum felt it was essential to undertake a subject in complete contrast to the grand purpose of *Gandhi*, to prevent a type-cast directing career. So in the summer of 1983 Attenborough went to New York to meet the film's producers, Cy Feuer and Ernest H. Martin, whose previous ventures into cinema had included *Cabaret*. He also saw the Broadway production and was again 'bowled over by the show, by its wonderful theatricality, the originality of its concept and, perhaps most impressive of all, by the discipline and commitment displayed by the entire company …

'That first evening on Broadway, I was immensely moved by several moments in the show. I remember particularly that when Maggie, one of the dancers, recalling her childhood, said, "Daddy, I would love to dance," tears rolled down my face in complete abandonment to sheer theatrical magic.'

The very theatricality of the show however made adaptation to another medium risky. In the original musical play by James Kirkwood and Nicholas Dante, Zach, a method-minded choreographer-director, is casting for a big Broadway musical. In selecting the final eight dancers from sixteen hopefuls, he asks them all to talk about their own lives and problems, which they do, with musical elaborations. His own personal life impinges with the arrival of Cassie, a former girl friend who walked out on him to go to Hollywood, but is now so desperate to work that she begs to join the chorus line.

Essential to the effect of the stage production was the illusion that the audience are actual spectators at this audition process. The difficulty, or impossibility, of creating a comparable illusion of participation for a cinema audience had already discouraged several other film directors: Mike Nichols and Sidney Lumet had already turned the project down as impractical. Attenborough however declared, 'The idea of being part of the world of the Broadway musical was irresistible to me. I absolutely adored it.'[37]

He acknowledged the problems: 'What worried me was that Michael Bennett's brilliant conception, of setting the action in the theatre and not departing from it at all, appeared intrinsic to its very success. What should the cinematic form be? Would a story set on a bare stage and in an empty auditorium satisfy a movie audience? Perhaps one ought to examine very carefully the possibility of moving away from the theatre and using the kids' revelations as narration for a series of illustrative flashbacks …

A Chorus Line (1986): Attenborough directs

'I had read Arnold Schulman's initial screenplay, and he had decided with some minimal exceptions to remain in the theatre. I thought some

of his dialogue adhered too strictly to the play and, in addition, was concerned that a certain number of what I'll call flashbacks might place the Bennett concept in jeopardy.'

After tortuous discussions with Feuer, Martin and Schulman, the conclusion was 'that our flashbacks, no matter what their subject matter, should also carry the sound of what is happening in the theatre. In this way, although they take longer for us to display than a mere flash in the character's recall, we always retain the atmosphere and tension of the actual audition.' In the end however all the flashbacks were discarded with the exception of those involving Zack and Cassie.

Aiming at a style of dance that would be more Hollywood than Broadway, Attenborough engaged 27-year-old Jeffrey Hornaday, who had choreographed *Flashdance*. The casting also stressed dance skills. In auditions in New York and Hollywood, some three thousand dancers were seen. This number resulted in a second call for four hundred, from whom the 129 dancers in the big opening sequence were selected. Of these, sixty were given screen tests – in full 35mm Panavision – to select the final chorus line of seventeen.

Filming in New York, Attenborough found himself working for the only time practically without any of his British familiars, except for the director of photography, Ronnie Taylor, and the editor, John Bloom, both of whom had won Oscars for their contributions to *Gandhi*. Diana Hawkins had the role and title of PR marketing director, but was already playing a much more positive role in production decisions. Attenborough worked very happily with the American crew, which included as production designer Patrizia von Brandenstein, an Oscar-winner for *Amadeus*.

Before principal photography began, on 1 October 1984, there were eight weeks of dance rehearsals – 'one of the most enjoyable experiences I've had in my life … They are a unique breed, these dancers/singers/actors/actresses. Indigenous and unique to the United States, they require themselves to have a compilation of all three disciplines. Inevitably, they may shine more in one than the others, but nevertheless the triumvirate of talent is assumed. They work phenomenally hard. Their preparation – dance classes, gymnasium work, voice training, and so on – is continually maintained within the constraints of working at their profession and they have an unqualified commitment to the job in hand.

A Chorus Line

'I forget what I had seen Michael Douglas in – not much because he had not done any of his major movies. I remember telling the executive producers that I was desperate to have this new star Michael Douglas, and being told by them that he couldn't act the skin off a rice pudding. These people have no concept about acting unless they can *see* the acting; and of course the best acting is always imperceptible. You are just aware of a reality, not of a performance.'

The schedule lasted sixteen weeks; and with the exception of two sequences the entire film was shot in the Mark Hellinger Theatre in New York. Attenborough recalled that the principal difficulty of the production was the monotony of shooting week after week in the same confined setting, with poor air conditioning, and with the same group of actors wearing the same costumes. Characteristically he combated the problem with 'a mixture of tomfoolery and informality'.

For some of the songs Attenborough dispensed with the traditional method of shooting to a pre-recorded track, preferring often to shoot and record directly; using the result as the guide track for the final sound in the film. 'This way you can capture the initial vitality and spontaneous reality of the performance – a quality you cannot recreate to playback.'

He also attempted to offset the dangers of visual monotony with occasional camera virtuosity – like the opening 'pigeon shot', with the camera apparently flying back and away over the heads of the dancers. The final scene – a huge Busby Berkeley ensemble performing 'One' –

is also a major departure from the stage original. Attenborough appears to have had to use all his powers of persuasion to convince Embassy Pictures and Feuer and Martin, as producers, that the sequins and gold satin and very considerable cost of this final scene were justified.

Chorus Line, rooted in the physicality of the theatre, was a near-unconquerable challenge to a film maker. Perhaps no other director could have been better equipped than Attenborough, with his life-long attachment to the stage and the communicated affection and sympathy he feels for the young hopefuls of the story. He was disappointed at the critical reception in America, but certainly not discountenanced: '*A Chorus Line* was difficult, but I think I brought it off.

'The American reviews were diabolical – the worst I have ever had as a director. The exception was Clive Barnes. He was dance critic at the time, but he persuaded his paper to let him do a film review. He wrote that *Chorus Line* was probably the best transference of a theatre musical into the concept of cinema, and went on to trounce "my idiot colleagues who do not know what dance is about". A staggering review. Overall, the reviews in Britain were much more generous than those in America.'

CRY FREEDOM

It was inevitable that Attenborough's anger against Apartheid should eventually find expression in film. He had optioned several scripts on South Africa over the years, and worked for a time – long before *Gandhi* – on an Apartheid story called *God is a Bad Policeman*. In the experiences and the books of the South African journalist Donald Woods he finally found his subject.

In the 1970s Woods was editor-in-chief of a South African newspaper, *The East London Daily Despatch*. Like many white liberals at the time he was sceptical about Steve Biko, whose Black Consciousness Movement he attacked as 'racist'. After meeting Biko however his views changed. The two men became friends; and when Biko died as a result of terrible injuries suffered in police custody, Woods campaigned, through editorials and speeches, to expose the truth about his murder – the government claimed that he had died as a result of a hunger strike.

In October 1977 Woods was arrested en route to a speaking engagement in the United States, and 'banned' (as Biko himself had been) – forbidden to travel, write, speak publicly or associate with more than one person at a time, outside his immediate family.

He determined to escape abroad, and crossed the border disguised as a priest, with his white hair dyed black. Reunited with his wife and five children abroad, he eventually reached London, and despite the continuing threats of the South African secret police, published his book *Biko*.

Woods, as Attenborough later pointed out,[38] was a much more complex and more powerful spokesman against Apartheid than the conventional crusading journalist of movies:

'Donald is a white, fifth-generation, English-speaking South African. He comes from a society where white children absorb racism from the moment of their birth and where most of them grow up genuinely believing they are inherently superior to the black majority.

'It is relatively easy for those of us born outside South Africa to condemn these attitudes. In my own case it required no leap of the imagination, since hatred of racism in all its forms was instilled from a very early age by my parents. But Donald Woods had no such role models on which to pattern his liberal beliefs. As a young man, in fact, he supported apartheid. It took a certain amount of bravery, as a mature adult, to admit he had been wrong. But the true nature of Donald's courage was not put to the test until he was in his forties, married, with five young children …

'He and his family came to England virtually penniless with only one suitcase of clothes and possessions among the seven of them …

'Most of us, if we are thinking, sensate people, have moral convictions of one kind or another. But how many, I wonder – myself included – would be prepared to sacrifice our entire lifestyle, all our creature comforts, for such a cause?'

A number of film producers in Britain and America showed interest in *Biko* and also in Woods' account of his own adventures, *Asking for Trouble*. Carl Foreman, Attenborough's producer and writer on *Young Winston*, optioned *Biko* and for several years tried to interest the American majors. All in turn passed on the subject: American and British commercial interests in South Africa made the theme too controversial. A deal with Columbia failed because the studio would not grant Attenborough and the Woods script approval.

This option expired in 1983, the year *Gandhi* was released. Woods considered Attenborough the ideal director for the subject, but decided that 'having done the story of a political martyr in a distant country, he would hardly want to follow up with the story of another political martyr in another distant country'. He heard however that Attenborough had read *Biko*; and was persuaded to send him a copy of *Asking for Trouble*. In August 1983 Attenborough told him that he was more than interested in the project. The special attraction was that the Biko–Woods story provided the opportunity not only for a powerful dramatic indictment of

Cry Freedom (1987): the
reconstruction of the
1976 Soweto massacre

the workings of Apartheid, but also 'an illustration of racial reconcilia-
tion between individuals as well as in a wider sense a plea for universal
tolerance'.[39]

Paradoxically, given earlier, rooted resistance to Apartheid themes,
Cry Freedom[40] was financed with less difficulty than Attenborough's
earlier films. Frank Price, who had handled *Gandhi* at Columbia, had
now moved to Universal, and enthusiastically undertook to finance the
project the moment Attenborough submitted it to him. The Government
of Zimbabwe also invested to the extent of providing facilities.

Attenborough's first step was to go to South Africa, astonishing
Woods with the energy with which he tracked down a long list of widely
scattered contacts. His visit attracted the attention of the security police,
who overheard the phrase 'when shooting begins' while monitoring a
conversation between Attenborough and Winnie Mandela. This was
reported as evidence of Attenborough's connection with planned ANC
violence. A grotesquely distorted television report of the meeting forced
Attenborough and his wife, who had accompanied him on the trip, to
leave the country. This was only the start of a virulent campaign of
hostile propaganda.

Attenborough commissioned John Briley, the writer of *Gandhi*, to
work on a script. Woods recalls that a major writing problem was accu-
rately to reflect Biko's attitude to militant action. 'Ultimately we agreed

on a formula proposed by Attenborough in which it was obvious from the script that Biko was essentially a peace-loving man who worked for a South African solution which ideally would preclude violence, but that he wasn't a pacifist who ruled out armed struggle under all circumstances and that he was, in fact, in the mainstream of black resistance, which recognised the role and options of the ANC and PAC and regarded their leaders as national heroes in the fight against apartheid.'[41]

Attenborough and his regular production associate, Terence Clegg, settled on Zimbabwe, the former Rhodesia, for the four-month location shooting. The country provided landscape and architecture closely resembling South Africa, but was also dangerously close to that country. Throughout the location filming the fear of physical attack was very real, and close security arrangements were maintained. In its propaganda war, the South African government successfully aroused suspicion and hostility among Biko's own supporters, spreading damaging rumours about the bad intentions of Woods and Attenborough. Another strategy was to invite a foreign producer to make a rival film about Biko and to announce that he would have all cooperation from the South African government. This purely phoney project ended when the hapless director found his residence permit cancelled.

Inevitably there was also criticism that the two main roles were filled by American actors; but the choice of Kevin Kline and Denzel Washington as Woods and Biko, amply justified in the outcome, had not been made lightly. Around one hundred South African actors had been considered for the role of Biko, who was 'one of the brightest, most charismatic, intelligent and fascinating men ever born in South Africa … It was an extraordinarily difficult role to cast, particularly as Steve is very clear in modern memory and had a number of distinctive attributes. He was over six feet tall, very good looking, intelligent, dynamic and as charismatic as any major movie star. He had the ability in his relaxed manner to capture and hold an audience – be it twenty people in a room or a thousand in an assembly hall – with consummate ease.'[42]

Attenborough is skilled in recognising an actor's suitability for a part from his playing in very different roles from the one for which he is being cast. In these cases, he had been impressed by Washington's playing in A Soldier's Story (1984) and Kline's as Hamlet. Equally John

Cry Freedom: Denzel
Washington as Steve Biko

Thaw's familiar appearances as a sober English policemn in television
series hardly predicted the dimension of his performance as the devious
Police Minister Kruger in *Cry Freedom*. All three mastered with total
conviction the sounds and cadences of the South African accent.

Shooting began in Harare on 14 July 1986. Locations used there
included the High Court of Justice which served for the scenes of Biko's
cross-examination during the 1976 South African Students Organisation
trial. For the scenes of Woods' escape fom the country, the unit moved
to Bulawayo and Mutare. *Cry Freedom* demanded the same spectacular
crowd scenes as *Gandhi*. For the sequence of Biko's funeral an estimated 18,000 extras were assembled. Donald Woods noted that
Attenborough appeared quite unconcerned with the security threat and
his own exposure during the shooting of the sequence.

Some scenes required white Zimbabweans as extras; and on occasion
old 'Rhodesian' attitudes emerged, though the black-white confronta-
tions which threatened on such occasions never developed seriously.

According to Woods, many actual incidents of the story were omitted simply because they would have appeared too coincidental or contrived for dramatic effect. Even the pleasant detail that the postal inspector who chanced along to help Woods' crossing of the river was called Moses was factually true. Out of similar concern for demonstrable veracity, the make-up artist Wally Schneiderman was required to understate the wounds on Biko's body and the injuries inflicted on Woods' small daughter with a T-shirt treated with harmful chemicals by the security police.

Attenborough was concerned that the case against Apartheid should not be weakened by any invention or speculation, particularly in the matter of Biko's death. Specifically he was determined 'that we shouldn't have a scene showing Biko actually being beaten as we had no exact knowledge of the details. We knew he had been beaten, but not how or by how many attackers. Attenborough's attachment to fact was due not only to love of truth, but also to tactical considerations: he reasoned that if even one material inaccuracy could be challenged successfully, it would call into question the veracity of the entire film. 'We therefore re-enacted only what we knew to be fact: that Biko was taken handcuffed into the cell, and that he was later found lying on the cell floor in the condition shown, and what the doctor and Security Police colonel said according to their inquest evidence.'[43]

For both Attenborough and Woods, the main purpose of the film 'was that it should result in a new awareness in the world of the real nature of apartheid – that apartheid had depths of horror that the world was not yet aware of and that more had to be done by governments everywhere to unite to rid the human race of this scourge.'[44]

'Nobody else I know could have done it,' concluded Donald Woods.[45] 'The many months of diplomacy required in dealing with the various factions in the South African liberation struggle, the reserves of energy required to deal with obstacle after obstacle, the cruel accusations, destructive attacks, and campaign of damaging lies he had to put up with from certain quarters in South Africa; the physical strength and mental stamina needed to initiate, supervise and complete *Cry Freedom* – these manifold demands were of a scale and intensity few human beings could have coped with and withstood.'

Cry Freedom enjoyed an excellent press reception everywhere it was shown (it was banned after one day on South African screens, but played successfully throughout the country a year later). Many critics noted its structural inconsistency. In the first half the dominant figure is Biko and the political issue is foremost. After Biko's death and the shift of interest to Woods, the story of the escape becomes more of an adventure story, with Apartheid as a secondary theme. Despite some enthusiastic notices in the United States, box office results there were disappointing. Attenborough felt that Americans were reluctant to be reminded of their own racial traumas of the 1960s.

Attenborough's greatest satisfaction, inevitably, was to know that the film succeeded in positively influencing ideas and opinions. 'As I understand it, in one of the Scandinavian countries, West Germany and Japan, government policy was actually changed by *Cry Freedom*. Members of the governments of each of those countries admitted to me that they and most of their colleagues were ignorant of the immensity of the horror, and that their eyes were opened by seeing the movie.

'The late Donald Woods insisted that it had a major effect on the wavering whites in South Africa. I think it provided a rallying point for a melange of people who knew in their gut that something was wrong, and wanted to give voice to it but didn't quite know how. What happened was that groups of people almost unknowingly found themselves united by seeing *Cry Freedom*, which became the catalyst in making them want to do and say something about it.

'That certainly happened with people in the peace movement and the non violent movement throughout the world. *Gandhi* had had the same outcome. There are now sixty or seventy Gandhi Foundations, whose object is to assist in areas of the world where there is racial disharmony, or disenfranchisement. In parts of South London Gandhi Foundation members have actually helped end riots and plundering of property and threatening of Bangladeshi women. That has happened in quite a number of other areas too – there are branches in Southall, Leicester and Birmingham, as well as in other countries.

'It is what I hoped was inherent in what I do. I never want to make the kind of film whose impact ends when the audience leaves the cinema. I always wanted to make films that might change or at least focus people's views. Perhaps that is what I most want to do – to conjure up and delineate what was already there but never found its resonance and voice.'

'I believe passionately that one must send an audience out of the theatre believing disaster is not inevitable. I wanted any anti-apartheid film I made to be unequivocal in its condemnation. But it still had to demonstrate that a solution was possible.'[46]

*   *   *

The 1980s had also seen Attenborough fulfil two roles which were crucial to British film culture of the period. He was Deputy Chairman (from 1980) and then Chairman (1986–1992) of Channel Four Television, during its early best years under the uncompromising and inspired direction of Jeremy Isaacs, followed by the different dynamism of Michael Grade. In that period Channel Four was a central influence in the revival of British Cinema; though by the time Attenborough left, economic and political circumstances had already brought to an end the brief golden age of television that the channel represented.

From 1981 to 1992 – an unprecedented length of tenure – he was a very active Chairman of the British Film Institute. His early years and the directorship of Antony Smith saw the celebration of the Institute's half century; the opening of the Museum of the Moving Image, whose then revolutionary innovations in museum techniques attracted world-wide acclaim; and the completion of the Paul Getty Conservation Centre at Berkhamstead, still the finest film archival facility in Europe. The munificence of the late Paul Getty not only assured these two achievements but also the Institute's removal to more suitable premises in Stephen Street. When he left in 1992, Attenborough could also point to a flourishing and innovatory production department, and the expansion of the regional film theatre enterprise. 'The BFI', he said, 'is no longer seen as solely metropolitan but as a magnificent institution progressively serving the whole country, now happily including Northern Ireland'.[47]

Attenborough's particular concern was that the holdings of the BFI should be more 'accessible'; and he opposed a 'snobbish, elitist attitude towards the cinema' and 'apparent concentration on the academic and the erudite as an end in itself'. He sought to heighten public and official consciousness of the cinema and of the Institute itself, and to make the organisation 'a voice and sounding board for those who work creatively within our industry… If I have done anything in these ten years or so I hope it has been to guide it to a conscious stature, a position where it is concerned and consulted whenever something important happens in the cinema.'

Sadly the years which followed Attenborough's departure saw many of his hopes for the BFI dashed. Subsequent managements have struggled to maintain adequate levels of funding, in a climate seemingly ever more hostile to expansion – and even maintenance – of activities. The Museum of the Moving Image was closed in 1999, and plans for an ambitious new Film Centre to house the BFI's varied activities are yet to be realised. The BFI's role in production has ceased, having been transferred to the UK Film Council; and its regional activities have yet to have the impact outside London which Attenborough envisaged, with the major responsibility for exhibition development again assumed by the UK Film Council, which has taken over the DCMS's funding and supervisory responsibility for the BFI. The Institute has yet to regain the stability afforded by the Attenborough years. Demands on its resources – particularly those of the National Film Archive – in a period of exploding audio-visual activity leave the twenty-first-century administration with a challenging task of reconstruction after the disappointments and difficulties of the immediate post-Attenborough years.

CHAPLIN

Attenborough's project for a film about Thomas Paine, the 18th century Anglo-American humanitarian and republican, has occupied him as long, and almost as passionately, as *Gandhi*. By 1988 a script, by Trevor Griffiths, was ready. Attenborough was confident that the film would soon go ahead as part of a three-picture deal he then had with Universal Pictures. When Universal finally decided not to proceed, saying that the required budget, some $50 million, was out of the question, Attenborough was devastated. Diana Hawkins, by this time his partner, looked for another project 'that would arouse a similar degree of compulsion in him. I decided it should be a biography, because that is what Dick most enjoys. It had to be someone who in some way had changed the society of his time. And then I wondered why we had never thought of Chaplin. Dick has worshipped him since he was a boy.'[48] (Coincidentally, Diana Hawkins had a family link with Chaplin. Her father Maurice Carter, a distinguished production designer, had been engaged by Chaplin to design his last, never-realised film project *The Freak*.)

In his book *In Search of Gandhi*, Attenborough recalls being taken by his father to see *The Gold Rush* when he was nine. 'He told me I would witness a genius in the relatively new medium of the cinema. He said he had never before seen a performer with this unique quality, an ability to make his audience both laugh and cry almost at the same instant, presenting "the common man" battling against circumstances which often seemed beyond his control and yet managing to overcome them.' In the 1980s Attenborough had been active in trying to set up a Chaplin Foundation and Museum in London – a project which was to be taken up again by the British Film Institute in 2002.

Since Chaplin's death in 1977 his widow had turned down quite literally hundreds of requests for the film rights in Chaplin's autobiography and in the Tramp costume (which is still protected by copyright). 'For a time', recalled Pam Paumier, then president of the company which operates the Chaplin artistic properties, 'we were refusing two or three requests every day. But Oona recognised that sooner or later a film would be made. And since she knew Richard Attenborough, and admired *Gandhi*, she finally decided in his favour. Her only condition was that she should NOT have approval of the script. She didn't want to see it. She was content to trust Attenborough's taste and judgment.'[49] The other source for the script was the present writer's *Chaplin, His Life and Art*, for which Lady Chaplin had permitted access to the vast Chaplin archives, with their extraordinary revelations of Chaplin's working methods.

Diana Hawkins, who was to be associate producer on the film, wrote the original screen story, which covered practically the entire life of Chaplin, from his first stage appearance at the age of five to his return to the United States at 83, to receive an honorary 'Oscar'; and this would remain the scope of the finished film. Attenborough's old collaborator Bryan Forbes made the first attempt to compress this great time-span into a manageable script. A subsequent version by William Boyd, the Scottish-born novelist and screenwriter, was ready by February 1991 when Universal, who had undertaken pre-production with apparent enthusiasm, planned to begin shooting. It was at this stage that Universal, evidently unnerved by the financial failure of Sydney Pollack's *Havana*, and unwilling to accept Robert Downey Jr, whom Attenborough was determined should play the leading role, put the project in turnaround. Sets which had cost millions of dollars and months of work were either dismantled and stored or left standing under security guard, in hope that production might be resumed under other auspices.

Other auspices materialised immediately. Mario Kassar of Carolco expressed his keenness to take over the project, though the negotiations – particularly extrication from the Universal involvement – were to be uncomfortably prolonged. As later events proved, Carolco's financial situation was more precarious than was evident from the company's bold investments in *Terminator II* during the early part of 1991. Only in the autumn, when the blockbuster box-office success of *Terminator II* was certain, was the finance for Chaplin finally assured, through a Franco-Italian-Japanese-American venture partnership.

The delay was in fact an advantage in allowing time to assess and revise the script. Boyd had successfully contained the Chaplin story within a two and a half hours' running time. In the interim period Tom Stoppard – uncredited – contributed some dialogue; and finally William Goldman, famous as a dramaturgical wizard, and a close friend since *A Bridge Too Far* and *Magic*, made some structural revisions. Goldman's principal contribution, developing an idea of Attenborough's, set the story in the framework of discussions between the aged Chaplin and the editor of his autobiography. This device, simple enough in itself, provided an extra dimension – Chaplin's own reassessment of earlier actions and opinions.

The casting of the main role was critical. Attenborough had looked at scores of actors during the three-year preparation period. A number of well-known stars, including Dustin Hoffman, Robin Williams and Billy Crystal, had declared their enthusiasm for this difficult but enviable role. Attenborough tested stars and unknowns, Americans as well as British (Chaplin was, of course, a Londoner). The final, surprise choice was 26-year-old Robert Downey Jr, a rising 'brat-pack' star with a history of high living and a record of interesting performances in a score of unremarkable Hollywood pictures. Downey proved in private to be innocent, intense, good-natured and vulnerably impressionable. He was touching and sometimes comic in his striving to achieve spiritual communion with Chaplin; fairly patient with the tedious eight hours of make-up work required for his appearance as the 70- and 80-year-old Chaplin; and under Attenborough's direction a phenomenally versatile and resourceful actor.

Shooting on *Chaplin* (the working title *Charlie* was eventually changed because of the similarity to the title of Cliff Robertson's *Charly*) finally began on 14 October 1991 in California. Two weeks earlier, Oona Chaplin had died in Switzerland.

Attenborough was as usual meticulous, almost obsessive, about the historical background. His production designer was once again Stuart Craig, whose team of art directors, set decorators and property people were fascinated by the cameras, the lights, the fashions, the tennis rackets, the habits and the trivia of Chaplin's Hollywood. A particular delight for the construction people was re-inventing the mechanism for the rocking hut in *The Gold Rush*. Another Attenborough regular and *Gandhi* Oscar-winner, the costume designer John Mollo, was joined by Ellen Mirojnick, who scoured American costume stores for authentic period clothing.

The background for the film's American scenes affords a panorama of Hollywood during four decades, between 1914 and 1952. Chaplin's own studio still stands, preserved as a monument, on a lot bordered by Sunset Boulevard, La Brea and DeLongpre. When Chaplin built the studio in 1918 the area was still a rural, residential suburb; and to assuage the locals' justified suspicion of movie folk, he designed the exterior, 'tastefully', as a fantasy impression of an English village, with little one-storey timbered buildings.

When *Chaplin* was made, the studio was occupied by A. & M. Records. The back-lot had been sold off, and the streets around are now built up and hectic with traffic – quite unlike Chaplin's early days there. Stuart Craig was thus obliged to recreate the studio completely, from the original architects' plans, among the orange groves of Fillmore, an hour's drive north of Hollywood.

No comparable plans of Mack Sennett's Keystone studios (where Chaplin's film career began) survive, though a few contemporary photographs give an idea of the external appearance. Craig's approach to recreating Keystone was to put himself in the position of a producer setting up in 1912. Undoubtedly he arrived at the same conclusions, and encountered some of the same technical problems – like the engineering difficulties of erecting a superstructure for an open stage out of timber that was inclined to warp and twist inconveniently. The ultimate compliment to Craig's re-invention came from William James, who, as Little Billy Jacobs, was Keystone's child star in 1913, before Chaplin's arrival there. Visiting the set, Mr Jacobs gazed in awe, exclaiming: 'It is just as I remember it. It is given to few men to have their memories realised.'

Restaging scenes from Chaplin's films on these open-air stages, the

Chaplin (1992) with
Geraldine Chaplin, who
plays her paternal
grandmother

1991 film crew experienced problems their precursors had faced three
quarters of a century before – the caprices of the Californian weather,
and the manipulation of the muslin blinds which in those early days had
to be stretched across the tops and sides of the stages to diffuse the
sunlight.

Of the many Hollywood period locations used in the film, the most
nostalgic was the old Los Angeles Theatre on Broadway – one of the last
great movie palaces, designed by S. Charles Lee in 1931. Chaplin
himself invested some money in the theatre in order that it could be
ready to open with the world première of *City Lights*. In 1992 the theatre
was marooned in one of the roughest parts of the city, offering its
patrons three horror-and-gore films for three dollars. For a day, deco-
rated for the production with flowers, flood-lights, tuxedos and evening
dresses, it was brought back to its old glory.

Other nostalgic moments of the Californian shooting were provided
by visitors to the set. The son and grandson of Chaplin's faithful cameraman Rollie Totheroh were regularly there and appear in the film as
camera assistants to the screen Rollie, played by David Duchovny. The
son of Loyal Underwood – the tiny character actor who played in so
many Chaplin films – came to the set, as did the daughter of Billie
Ritchie, one of Chaplin's fellow-artists in the Karno music hall companies. Ritchie's widow had made trick costumes at the studios for many
years. Chaplin's English cousin cried with nostalgia when she saw the

recreation of the Chaplin studio she had known well. With other Chaplin enthusiasts seizing the chance to work as extras, the Californian set became a kind of full-time Chaplin fan club.

The casting of a necessarily episodic film followed the usual Attenborough style, with one-scene roles allotted impartially to stars and to unknowns. In somewhat more extensive parts, Dan Aykroyd was cast as an expectorating Mack Sennett and Kevin Kline – strikingly different from his role in *Cry Freedom* – as the swashbuckler king of twenties Hollywood, Douglas Fairbanks. Geraldine Chaplin, with remarkable intensity of feeling, played her own grandmother, Hannah, who lost her

Geraldine Chaplin and Robert Downey Jr in *Chaplin*

reason while Chaplin was still a child. Attenborough considered Anthony Hopkins's performance as Chaplin's editor, 'exquisite'; and was also very pleased with Moira Kelly in the dual role of Chaplin's last wife, Oona, and his first teenage love, Hetty Kelly.

So far as actors' commitments permitted, Attenborough mostly shot the film in continuity, except that the early scenes, set in London, had to be filmed at the end. Again Craig attempted a meticulous recreation of the London of the turn of the century – the poor streets and music halls. The music halls were authentic – Wilton's, the earliest surviving purpose-built music hall in Britain, dating from 1858, and the Hackney Empire, a massive, ornate theatre from 1901 and the apogee of the variety era.

The streets that Chaplin knew are gone or changed beyond recognition. Again Craig, a production designer of ambition that awes producers (who unkindly nickname him 'Gi'-us-a-million Craig') recreated a whole street complex behind King's Cross railway station. For weeks it was the spectacle of the neighbourhood, the most ambitious film set built in Britain for many years.

The final scenes – the linking sequences involving the book editor, played by Anthony Hopkins – were shot at Chaplin's own home in Corsier sur Vevey, Switzerland. Chaplin's former butler, Mario, played his real-life role. As a location the Manoir de Ban was inconvenient. The Swiss weather in early February was unhelpful, and for the only time in a production that ran like Swiss clockwork, the shoot went over schedule. Cautious counsels had from the start argued to shoot the scenes in the studio; but for Attenborough there was clearly an irresistible romantic motive in filming at the Manoir de Ban – a special sense of keeping faith with Chaplin. Most important, he says, 'there was an additional spur to Downey in facing the challenge of the reality of this setting, Chaplin's own home, the place where he lived and died'.

'My wish', he said before the release of the film, 'is that people will come away from *Chaplin* with a greater feeling for what a wonderful medium the cinema is; a deeper understanding of the human foibles and frailties exemplified in this man who was a genius; and the reasons why he finds himself at such odds with what is accepted as proper and appropriate behaviour'.

His wish was not to be granted. The press on both sides of the

Atlantic was generally so hostile that the film's audience was seriously restricted. The antagonism was excessive; *Chaplin*'s merits are enough to fascinate audiences on the rare occasions when it is now revived. The film's unconquerable handicap was the attempt to contain the entire life story in 145 minutes, and the reception was not helped by the circumstances of the film's release. *Chaplin* was selected for the Royal Film Performance, which meant that it was first reviewed in Britain, whose critics at that time were notoriously hostile to Chaplin. Hence many of the notices were directed at the subject rather than the film: one national review began, 'As everyone knows, Charlie Chaplin was a very unpleasant man indeed …'

When the British dealt so harshly with their own – Attenborough as well as Chaplin – it seemed to licence open season when the film opened in the United States. 'This is a disappointing, misguided movie', wrote Roger Ebert in the *Chicago Sun-Times*, 'that has all of the parts in place to be a much better one. Robert Downey Jr. succeeds almost uncannily in playing Chaplin; the physical resemblance is convincing, but better is the way Downey captures Chaplin's spirit, even in costume as the Tramp. The production values are impressive, the period sets are meticulously convincing, the supporting actors are generally very good, especially Geraldine Chaplin, playing her own grandmother; Kevin Kline, as Douglas Fairbanks, and James Woods, as Chaplin's attorney.'[50]

One of the film's kindest critics, James Berardinelli's *Reelviews* wrote: 'It's easy to pick out the single major flaw of *Chaplin*. The narrative is too ambitious. Attempting to condense seventy-eight years into one hundred and forty-four minutes is a Herculean task that defeats a director of even Richard Attenborough's accomplishments. There's too much material, and, because the story is so rich, characters and events go whizzing by at dizzying speeds. *Chaplin* becomes a series of scenes and images rather than a cohesive whole.'[51] *Sight and Sound* gave it fair credit as 'a film that is always watchable, and always manages to stay the right side of hagiography'.[52]

BEFORE THE CAMERAS AGAIN

Between post-production and release of *Chaplin*, Attenborough accepted his first acting assignment for thirteen years, in Steven Spielberg's *Jurassic Park*. (Two years earlier he had considered the part of Smee, eventually played by Bob Hoskins, in Spielberg's *Hook*.) Attenborough and Spielberg had first met ten years earlier when *Gandhi* and *ET* were both nominated for the Directors' Guild Award. The night before the event the Attenboroughs had seen *ET*, loved it, and convinced themselves that *Gandhi* had no chance. 'So when Clint announced my name, I was certain he had made a mistake, got the wrong card or something.' Instead of going to the podium, Attenborough went to the table where Spielberg was sitting, and declared tearfully, 'Mr Spielberg, this is a dreadful miscarriage of justice! *ET* should have had this award.' He insists that this was no calculated theatrical gesture. 'I truly felt that. But I took the award, and later Spielberg said that he didn't need an Oscar, because Attenborough had already given him one!

'While I was still working on *Chaplin*, he took me to breakfast at the Dorchester – wearing his baseball cap – and said (I'm sure he was pretending) that he had come over specifically to persuade me to go back to acting. He asked me if I had read *Jurassic Park* (which I hadn't) and said there was this mad genius character, and until he had cast Hammond he did not know how to cast the rest of the picture. So I said, as Olivier had said to me when I asked him to do *Oh! What a Lovely War*, that if he asked me to read the telephone directory I would feel flattered. So it was done there and then. The character was changed somewhat: in Crichton's book he is a mean capitalist, but I gave him a soft and gentle (and maybe somewhat suspect) Scottish accent and a genial appearance, which I hoped hinted at an extra dimension.

Attenborough as Kriss
Kringle in *Miracle on
34th Street* (1994)

'Spielberg is a genius, and not in any way arrogant. He comes on the set with everything planned, but though he is wonderfully confident he is quite capable of going into a brown haze and scrapping three hours' work if it doesn't satisfy him. He was enchanting to me, though I must have caused him great anxiety and angst and anger. I travelled from Britain overnight, and went straight from the plane to the studio to start work. Not surprisingly, perhaps, on the set I kept drying, which is very rare for me, because I work very hard on my lines. It must have taken fifteen takes, but he never gave me an iota's indication that I was causing him a problem.

'When he was making *Schindler's List* he asked me to take over the direction for a week – he was having trouble with the special effects for *Jurassic Park* I think. I had been in Los Angeles, and we had looked at tests for *Schindler's List* together; so I knew the subject and I had read the script. But I was absolutely caught up in my own film at the time, so I simply could not. I would love to have contributed to that film. When we set up a centre for German-Jewish research – the whole question of the holocaust – at the University of Sussex, Steven financed it.'

In 1994 Attenborough recreated Edmund Gwenn's original role of Kris (now re-named Kriss) Kringle, the department store Santa Claus who comes to look very much like the real thing, in Les Mayfield's remake of George Seaton's 1947 *Miracle on 34th Street*. Philip Strick, in *Sight and Sound,* wrote that 'the weight of the story has been shifted to the shoulders of Richard Attenborough whose zest for perilous magic seems unclouded by the recollection of a few undisciplined dinosaurs. His celebrity status and impermeable jolliness, while never quite other-worldly enough, render him the ideal Santa Claus, a creature of popular, and mercenary, fiction with any number of good deeds to his name.'[53] Though his own notices were enthusiastic, the film was uninspired, and Attenborough was disappointed in the result: 'It was a good perform-ance, and a very credible performance in an incredible part really. I did one or two scenes quite well. But because it was not far from my own persona in terms of bonhomie it did not get the credit.' At least however it gave him the distinction of leading Macy's Christmas Parade.

He was to resume the role of John Hammond in *The Lost World: Jurassic Park* (1997) and, having rediscovered the taste for acting, he accepted a succession of supporting roles – the English Ambassador in Kenneth Branagh's all-star *Hamlet* (1996), a very human Lord Burghley in Shekhar Kapur's *Elizabeth* (1998), Jacob in *Joseph and the Amazing Technicolor Dreamcoat* (1999), starring Donny Osmond; and the Old Gentleman in Catherine Morshead's graceful, made-for-TV *The Railway Children* (2000). He played Magog the Arbiter in the American-made Henson miniseries *Jack and the Beanstalk: The Real Story* (2001), and 'the writer-director' in Terence Ryan's forgettable adaptation of Spike Milligan's *Puckoon* (2002).

Attenborough remains fascinated by the tools and techniques of the actor, and would probably still enjoy the stage. 'I would love to have done Shylock, but I wouldn't risk any of the great classical parts now. At my age you cannot trust your memory; and I am always terrified of drying. Of course if I could possibly remember the lines, what I would most love to do is *The Tempest* – that last speech!'

SHADOWLANDS AND SCREEN ACTING

In 1993, having passed his half-century in pictures, Attenborough made the film which brought him the most unanimous praise of his career. In his own terms, 'When people ask me which film I am most proud of, I can truthfully say that this is the one I am least ashamed of – well not ashamed, but least embarrassed. It emanated from as good a script as I have ever worked on – if not necessarily the best: Jack Briley's script for *Gandhi* was remarkable in containing the subject, as was Bill Goldman's for *A Bridge Too Far.*'

William Nicholson's screenplay is based on the true story of the autumnal romance and marriage of the Oxford don and best-selling author C. S. Lewis and an American divorcee, Joy Gresham, who began their acquaintance with a fan letter. The screen version, wrote Roger Ebert, 'has found two perfect actors to play this unlikely couple, Anthony Hopkins and Debra Winger. He is shy sometimes to the point of being tongue-tied; he nods and hems and haws and looks away, and retreats behind formulas of courtesy. She is more direct, an outspoken woman who sometimes surprises him by saying out loud what they have both been thinking, but that he would never have said. She sees at a glance the comfortable rut he is in – the dinners at his college dining hall, the evenings in front of the fire, reading while the wireless provides classical music from the BBC. She isn't out to "catch" him. It's more that he discovers he cannot imagine her going away.

'Their courtship is an odd one. He issues invitations lamely, as if sure she will not accept. He is so terrified of marriage that he has to couch his proposal in "practical" terms – if he marries her, she will not be forced to leave Britain. She has to negotiate the clouded waters of university politics, the annual dinners of the college head, the curiosity and pointed questions of his nosy colleagues. When it comes to sex, he hasn't a clue, and she talks him through it: "What do you do when you go to bed?" "I put on my pajamas and say my prayers and get under the covers." "Well, then, that's what I want you to do right now, except that when you get under the covers, I'll be there."

'Lewis has been confident in his writings and lectures that he knows the purpose of suffering and pain: It is God's way of perfecting us, of carving away the wrong parts, of leaving a soul ready to enter heaven. But when Joy contracts cancer, when she finds herself in terrible pain, he finds he is not at all sure of his theory. And, facing the possibility that they will be parted, together they create an idea of human life on earth that comforts him more than his theories.'

The play had begun life on BBC television in 1985, when the parts of C. S. Lewis and Joy Gresham were played by Joss Ackland and Claire Bloom. The production received the International Emmy as well as BAFTA awards for Claire Bloom and for best television play. In the stage version at the Queen's Theatre, Shaftesbury Avenue in 1989, the roles were played by Nigel Hawthorne and Jean Lapotaire. The film project was brought to Attenborough by the television producer Brian Eastman, who shared producer credit with Attenborough.

'Nigel Hawthorne was wonderful in the role on stage, but the picture was not mountable with him – he had not yet made *The Madness of King George.* Tony Hopkins accepted at once.

'I knew from the start who I wanted to play the woman, but everyone warned me that Debra Winger was very difficult. I said, "We'll have to deal with that – she's a supreme and beautiful actress and perfect for this part." I met her in Los Angeles. And we had a very good talk and then I said, "Now, Miss Winger, you have a …" And she said, "Oh, I know I have a reputation. It's all a lot of cock." … "Well I assure you it is quite a reputation." "I don't give a ******* **** about all this. All I care about is the quality of the work. You make great movies and you'll get great performances. I'll be fine." "Well I can tell you here and now if you're not fine I'll know within 48 hours and I shall recast." … "That's

Shadowlands (1993):
Anthony Hopkins and
Debra Winger

a deal." She never gave me a moment's trouble. Her dedication, devo-
tion, commitment to the subject was unequalled and unequivocal. I
remember when she left, watching her walk from the hotel and she just
walked like Joy Gresham. I think those two performances were as good
as any two performances I had ever been connected with.

'The fascinating problem for me was that here you had two actors
who work in totally opposed methods. Anthony Hopkins clearly agrees
with Ken Loach, who wrote in a recent article that rehearsing in the
cinema is a highly questionable function, because the cinema gives you
opportunities that you do not have in the theatre of capturing the one-
off magical moment, determined by intuition, not by study. Tony
Hopkins doesn't like rehearsal at all. He has convinced himself that too
much rehearsal robs the dialogue of its spontaneity, and that it only really
works if you can get it very quickly. When you are working with him,
although he doesn't put off the other actors, he will say all sorts of things
in rehearsal which are wholly appropriate but which are not what is written in the script. That doesn't mean that when he comes to the take his
words are not perfect. But he almost prefers to shoot straight away, once
you've done the technical rehearsal.

'Now Miss Winger is the antithesis. She likes to rehearse and
rehearse and rehearse – and it doesn't seem to damage her performance
or in any way take away the freshness. But for the director, working with

Shadowlands: Anthony Hopkins and Joseph Mazzello

this duo was something of a problem. I very often used to walk through Tony's part with Debra so that she would have a lot of time rehearsing in advance; and only at the last moment would I put in Tony for one rehearsal with her; and it worked, and brought out the best in both of them. Tony is so unchallengeable in his reality. Debra just melted in front of him – and vice versa. They thought each other tremendous.

'The acting which I admire most in the cinema is a kind of under-acting, the kind of performance where it is a monstrous insult to suggest it is actually being *performed* at all. Hence I adore Spencer Tracy. For me there has to be a reality that makes you oblivious that there is acting. But I fear in large measure those performances which receive the most acknowledgements are those where you can *see* the acting. Anthony Hopkins does a wonderful characterisation in *Remains of the Day,* but for me his performance in *Shadowlands* is infinitely superior. You see the real processes of that person, not the acting. In the same way, when I won the BAFTA Award for *Guns at Batasi* I knew it was to a large extent because of the make-up work on my nose and my gold teeth. With all that, you could see I was acting! But the best things I have done, like *The Dock Brief* or *Séance on a Wet Afternoon,* I hope you *don't* see the acting.

'I had some of my first and best lessons about screen acting almost sixty years ago, when I worked for six or seven days with Edward G.

Robinson, whom I adored and whose memory I still adore, on *Journey Together* (1945). He talked to me a lot. He was a great stage actor also of course; and he told me, 'I don't denigrate the theatre. I've done masses of stage work. But in the theatre you can get away with anything. While in the cinema, to be superb you have to be really superb.' He said that it was absolutely imperative in acting for the screen that there must be nothing on your mind other than the circumstances of the screen person, whom you shouldn't have to think about because you have characterised him. Your mind has to be absolutely concentrated on what that person is experiencing – their various thoughts and emotions at that particular moment of the story.

'In those days, sixty years ago, it was harder than now. The screen actor had to be absolutely precise on his moves, to stay on his marks and within camera range and focus. There were bits of wood battened to the floor as markers, so that you could feel them with your feet. But, Robinson said, "your lines have to be so firm in your head that you can afford to throw them away and then call them back as if they were new and spontaneous. If you cannot do that, this remarkable instrument that is recording you *will not photograph your thoughts*. But if you're right", he said, "it will do just that."'

IN LOVE AND WAR

B y contrast the later 1990s brought two critical and commercial debacles; yet both *In Love and War* and *Grey Owl*, in the retrospective view, are films of substantial merit which, flawed though they may be in different ways, in no way deserved the disdain and relegation which was their fate. *In Love and War* is based on the published reminiscences of Henry Villard, who was a participant in a real-life First World War romantic drama involving the young Ernest Hemingway, and which Hemingway himself recalled in his brief and bitter *A Very Short Story*. As a cocky, ambitious 18-year-old reporter, Hemingway arrives in Northern Italy in 1918, as Italian forces are being pressed by a massive Austrian advance. Rushing into the thick of the action, he impetuously attempts to rescue a fatally wounded Italian soldier, and himself receives serious

In Love and War (1996): Chris O'Donnell and Sandra Bullock

injuries. He is saved from having his leg amputated by the efforts of a
26-year-old American nurse, Agnes von Kurowsky. After an initially
uneasy relationship – Ernest is brash, Agnes is cautious – they recognise
their mutual love, which is briefly consummated in the unlikely setting
of the local brothel. Hemingway is repatriated to the United States.
Agnes accepts the proposal of a rich and charming Italian doctor, but
thinks better of it, returns to the United States, and seeks out
Hemingway. Bitter, proud and disillusioned, he rejects her. The film's
end titles tells us that Agnes distinguished herself as a nurse, and
survived to a great age. Hemingway became a great writer, married four
times, and shot himself at 62. The witness to all this is the gentle Villard,
deeply but hopelessly in love with Agnes.

The film undoubtedly has a script problem, a failure of integration
between the intimate story and the vast dramatic landscapes of the war
against which it is set. Without now remembering the details,
Attenborough recalls unresolved difficulties over the script with the
producers, Dimitri Villard and New Line. 'If only they'd left us alone. If
they had allowed us to make the film we originally wanted to make, our
original script. But they have these ridiculous script doctors. They bring
in these people who write an analysis and then are given the right to
rewrite the screenplay, which they did in our case – I think three times.
I can't remember all the credits on it. I think it's true to say that your
skill or lack of is foretold and determined by the screenplay. All the best
scripts are by a single screenwriter. This terrible habit of having an office
block of writers that you call upon – the company, not the director, that
is – when you feel insecure before you go into production! It was one of
the rare subjects that did not originate with me. It was a New Line property and I was engaged as director and therefore I was not entirely my
own boss, and certainly not able to avoid the whims and critiques of
those who made the law of that company.

'It was a good subject though, with wonderful locations. This was the
first time I used digital special effects techniques. The scene of Austrian
troops coming over the mountain, which looked like 25,000, was
achieved with 50 men. It was sad to think that in this day and age
nobody will ever realise that for the beginning of *Gandhi* we had
400,000 real, living people.'

Attenborough's principal disappointment with the film's reception was the neglect of the undeniably fine performances of Sandra Bullock, Chris O'Donnell and, as Villard, the 23-year-old Mackenzie Astin, whose work till then had mainly been in television. 'I thought they gave the most beautiful performances – the entire ensemble. But not only did the critics not want to accept, in the first place, that Sandra Bullock is an excellent actress, but they want her to remain that persona, that kooky girl-next-door, that they all adored. And because Chris did not look or act like the mature Hemingway they dismissed him. They were not prepared to accept that this 18-year-old boy is not the Hemingway we know, but an embryo, with all the future still to be formed. They wanted the knowing foresight of the conventional biopic.'

One of the rare critics perceptive and conscientious enough to recognise the links with *Shadowlands* was Philip Kemp, in *Sight and Sound*: '[Attenborough's] latest work amplifies and develops very much the same themes. In fact the two films, taken together, dovetail perfectly, each illuminating and complementing the other. Both are about a writer faced with a traumatic love affair which brings him both joy and suffering. In the case of C. S. Lewis it comes late in life, at a time when he's ceased to expect it, and for all the agony it causes him, he survives as a warmer, deeper, far more human person, connected to life in a way he never was before. To Hemingway it comes too early, before he's able to handle it and makes him cut off a whole area of himself from the risk of intimacy, souring his emotional life and his response to women forever. "The hurt boy", Agnes' voice-over muses at the end of the film, "became an angry man", as we see the bitter disappointed features of the ageing writer. Love and suffering, these two films imply, may well be beneficial if they come when we're ready for them, but coming at the wrong time they can destroy us.'[54] His approval of the film led Kemp to the concession – unusual for an English critic – that perhaps, after all, Attenborough is an auteur.

GREY OWL

The *Grey Owl* project was initiated by Jake Eberts. Attenborough could hardly have hoped for a more intriguing subject for a screen biography. Gandhi, Churchill, Chaplin were titans. Archibald Stansfield Belaney was an equivocal and bewildering creature, at once idealist and fraud. Born in 1888, the illegitimate child of an alcoholic wastrel, he was brought up in Hastings by two maiden aunts. Emotionally bruised by this desertion by his parents, he found escape in caring for strange pets and in his fascination with native American culture. At 18 he left his job as a clerk to emigrate to Canada. Disappearing to North Ontario, he learned to canoe and trap and survive in the wilderness. He saw service with the Canadian army in the First World War; and thereafter seemed to have slipped his skin, transmuted into a native American. In this new persona he was accepted by the native American communities, and worked as a forest ranger and guide in Prince Albert National Park. A series of books, begun in 1931, brought him world celebrity and led to triumphant lecture tours in America and Europe, in which, as Grey Owl, he promoted a surprisingly modern environmentalist message: his impeccable credo was that we are the servants of the planet, not its masters. Only on his death in 1938 at the age of 50 did his millions of fans and followers learn the truth of his spectacular imposture and of Archie Grey Owl's several and bigamous relationships, which spawned at least four children.

The Attenborough brothers were among those whose lives were undoubtedly influenced by seeing Grey Owl when a British lecture tour took him to Leicester in 1936 – they were obliged to queue for several hours to get a seat. The Leicester lecture and the queues are recreated in the film.

Grey Owl (1999): Pierce Brosnan as Grey Owl and Annie Galipeau as Pony

William Nicholson's script had rich sources in Grey Owl's own books and a number of biographies. Perhaps learning from the lesson of *Chaplin*, the story is concentrated upon two years of Grey Owl's rise to fame, from his first impact upon National Park visitors, to his lectures to enthusiastic mass audiences. The spectator is invited to share with Grey Owl's original public the conviction that he is what he claims to be; only gradually does the mask begin to crack, as small incidents – an over-curious newsman; an old acquaintance who arrived with him in Canada; the return to Hastings – alert us to something more than meets the eye. Concentrating the action enables Nicholson to leave aside Grey Owl's more colourful romantic adventures: between 1917 and 1934 his on-and-off common-law wife was Gertrude Bernard, known as Anahareo, or, as in the film, 'Pony'. The film underlines a nice irony in the relationship. Pony, an authentic native American, is first seen as a spoilt kid in jodhpurs, who has to be initiated by Grey Owl, the imposter, into her own native culture and tradition. Nicholson's script is literate and subtle, full of equivocations appropriate to the subject: thus as we are disarmed by cute little beavers, we realise that this is not Attenborough's manipulation, but Grey Owl's own preco- cious way of seducing a 30s public, less exposed to the ecological message.

A fundamental and fatal flaw in the film is the casting of the undeni- ably charming Annie Galipeau in the role of Pony. 'The casting of the girl became a major question. The Los Angeles financiers were of course keen that I should have a Hollywood name, even if it meant that we

would have to darken her skin. But my conviction was that if you were
telling the story of a white man who darkened himself and was a phoney,
though totally convincing and captivating, to cast another phoney in the
role of the genuine native Indian girl was madness. I couldn't understand anyone even vaguely considering it.

'When the picture was originally due to start, I saw in a test a girl walk
across the screen and say one line. I thought she was marvellous, so we
brought her down from the north of the country – only to find she didn't
look a day over 14. So I said to her mum, who was with her, "Please
forgive me, etc., but we are not making *Lolita*. Of course if the film is
postponed …"

'And of course it was postponed, and we asked her back. I was totally
captivated by her. We tested her and we tested one or two other girls;
and everyone agreed she was the winner. She looked totally ravishing
and credible, and was the real thing – living in the outback, riding and
everything. The problem was that her native languages were French or
native Canadian, with hardly any English. In my conceit, I was
convinced that we could teach her – because her instincts were very
good. I never really reckoned with the fact that because she was always
translating into English, she could never get the colloquial flow of
dialogue. And consequently Pierce understandably found difficulty in
acting with her. I don't think that meant the performances were second-
rate – on the contrary I think that Pierce in particular was very good and
clever. But the scenes between them don't work as they should.

'And I was even more stubborn in refusing to re-voice her, as Pierce
wanted. I felt I owed so much to the child that I would not do it. Instead
I looped line after line with her, but it did not make any significant
difference. Although she looked divine and totally credible the scenes
didn't have the spontaneity they needed. That was my fault and no one
else's, and it mitigated against the credibility of the film.

'We also had a piece of pure bad luck, which crippled the structure
at a crucial moment. The big scene in the theatre at the end of the film
is preceded by a group of other dialogue sequences. To deal with this
and to relieve the concentration of dialogue, we interposed in the script
a big action scene of a battle in canoes, with some hunters going after
Grey Owl, to beat him up. We rehearsed this a great deal with sketch
artists and with stunt men, and were due to shoot it on the last Saturday

before we moved to a new location the following day. So we had to go with it that day, whatever the conditions of weather whatever. Everybody arrived at five o'clock in the morning, bags packed, checked out of the hotel, ready to move out at the end of the day.

'But at 6 and 7 and 8 the stunt guys who had rehearsed it all were not to be seen. Eventually we learnt that they were on another picture which had gone over schedule and that they had been paid a great deal of money to stay on there. So all I could do was to attempt to shoot the scene with crowd artists – not even crowd artists, but local people. It was so unsatisfactory and phoney that it was unusable. Hence the last reel of the film now lacks the dramatic line you always work for. That was not my fault – but it was part of the failure of the making of the movie. And I think those two elements together damaged *Grey Owl*.'

The press were merciless, almost totally precluding theatrical release for the film. Brosnan's sensitive and polished performance was written off in quips about '007 in ringlets'. There was little credit for some exquisite sequences, notably the comic, touching reunion of Archie Belaney and his Hastings aunts, beautifully played by Renee Asherson and Stephanie Cole. One of the rare appreciative reviews was Richard Falcon's in *Sight and Sound*: 'Brosnan is excellent in an unlikely role and the film abounds with genuine pleasures: director of photography Roger Pratt's shot of the tepees on the plain at night, lit from within like Chinese lanterns, gives you a sense of the romantic appeal the Canadian wilderness must have had for young Archie and goes some way to explaining why he left Hastings to live there. Then there's his return to Hastings where he visits his maiden aunts, a small gem of Alan Bennett-like understated insight. As the two old ladies reveal they have kept his room exactly as he left it, they add an apologetic rider: "I'm afraid we had to throw away the dead snakes."

Attenborough himself is again philosophically regretful at the dismissal of the film: 'What is sad is that very few people gave credence to a really extraordinary subject. This man was a truly remarkable figure, who stood for many things that I believe in: the honour of the native Canadians – the Red Indians – the fight against racial prejudice and the fight for the preservation of nature and living creatures of the earth. He made the most incredible impact. And very few of the reviews gave any credit to it, didn't recognise it at all. And that I think was a pity.'

WHAT NEXT?

The greatest annoyance of the undeserved dual debacle of *In Love and War* and *Grey Owl* is that it handicaps the financing of the next project. Attenborough's dream remains the Tom Paine biography, which would now require a budget of 60 to 70 million dollars. 'It would need a major company – it's too big a sum to raise on the street. And neither the project nor I are obvious box-office at the moment. I don't have any problem getting insurance, I'm glad to say. I am idiotically well and have not lost any of my energy. I don't have any desire to retire. The very idea is anathema. If I didn't wake in the morning at half past six and say "Wow! think what I've got to do today!" – then I would stop. But because I made these two failures – commercial and critical – I am not flavour of the month. In terms of current cinema and conventional box-office wisdom, I am old fashioned; I like a beginning, a middle and an end; I like narrative. The Tom Paine story is period; it's politics; it's biography; it's everything they don't want.

'But on the contrary, I am convinced that it could have a huge box-office attraction, say if Daniel Day-Lewis would play the part. I hope I could get Tony to play Ben Franklin; and Washington would be ideal for Michael Douglas or Martin Sheen. There is a fantastic girl's part; and a fine Meryl Streep character. With those actors you can start to talk.

'I want to do it more than anything else. I know the subject so well. And anyone who knows about Tom Paine will tell you he was the greatest Englishman that ever lived, truly the most extraordinary character. They know the scale of the thing and what one could do with it, and how commercially attractive it could be – passionate romance and the American War of Independence, crossing the Delaware and all that.'

While waiting for *Paine* he has been occupied with several major administrative projects. His involvement with the Centre for Disability and the Arts is passionate and formative. In 2002 he was appointed President of the Royal Academy of Dramatic Art – a post which had been discontinued after the death of its previous President, Princess Diana. Attenborough's presidency marks the culmination both of his intensely loyal sixty-year association with RADA, and of the restoration of its fortunes, thanks largely to his efforts.

'When Dame Edith Evans was President, it was decided that there should be a Chairman also – her voice and presence had its problems when it came to business meetings – and Felix Aylmer was appointed. I succeeded him at about the time that it became evident that the Academy was broke. We had no grants for drama students at all, so we had to pay for every child. The cowboy repair works that were done after the bombing in 1943 were coming undone. The roof was leaking. The electricity had been condemned. We were in a frightening situation.

'Then suddenly the lottery came; and the day after it went into oper- ation, we put in an application. After a lot of hooing and hahing they agreed to a budget of £32 million, £8 million of which we had to find ourselves, at the same time as we had to keep going and pay our way. Raising that money took around six or seven years, starting in 1993 or 1994. We finally opened eighteen months ago. It almost broke my back. Raising the money for *Gandhi*, and raising the money for RADA were the two toughest jobs I ever had.'

The Attenboroughs themselves were substantial donors to the fund; and as President, Attenborough is clearly far from finished with RADA, delighting as he does in the results, a state-of-the art complex linking the old Gower Street and Malet Street premises and providing a superb, endlessly adaptable theatre.

He is hardly less excited by the Dragon project, which involves the creation of a huge new studio complex on a 650-acre brownfield site in Wales, along with the hotels, hospital and other facilities that go with an international studio facility. Eventually there may also be a neighbouring movie theme park. Tortuous negotiations finally secured permission to build an exit to the M4, so as to provide road access to Heathrow in 100 minutes. 'The scheme was initiated by Stuart Villard, who is a Labour party supporter, mad about the movies, had done a certain amount of development and bought this site. He initially asked me if I would be a consultant, and of course I have become more and more involved, as have my regular associates: Terry Clegg is CEO and Diana Hawkins and my lawyer Claude Fielding are also deeply involved. The financing comes from Barclays' Bank. We plan to open at the beginning of 2005 …

'Once they start to build, I don't need to watch, and I can get on with other things. *Jurassic Park 4* is in preparation, and they want me to play in *The Snow Prince.* And as the next directorial project, I am hoping to set up *Closing the Ring,* with Shirley MacLaine in the lead …'

✻   ✻   ✻

'You know there's an America critic who is not a huge fan of mine. However, he paid me the compliment of which I am most proud – though I am sure he meant it derogatorily. He said something like: "The problem with Attenborough's work is that he is more interested in the content than the execution."

'Almost without exception that is true, I am glad to say. I am sorry if I am not more adventurous cinematically. I am sorry if it did not have innovative concepts. But my concern is always, did the film say what I wanted to express, or advocate? So, yes – he couldn't have paid me a nicer compliment.'

NOTES

1. *Richmond Herald*, 21 May 1949

2. *The Times*, 28 April 1963

3. Jonathan Hacker and David Price, *Take 10, Contemporary British Film Directors* (London, 1991)

4. All subsequent quotations from Attenborough, if not otherwise attributed, are from interviews with David Robinson in August 1992 and April–June 2003

5. Hacker and Price, *Take 10, Contemporary British Film Directors*

6. He is capable of staging little dramas if it can help an actor. On *Chaplin,* working with an actor who was having difficulty, he suddenly turned from their intimate discussion to yell angrily that the camera crew were making too much noise. The crew were shocked; Attenborough never yells and in any case they had been quite quietly discussing their business. Having apparently calmed the actor, Attenborough turned away and gave the camera crew a huge conspiratorial wink making it clear to them that the tantrum had been staged, a subtle psychological trick to shift the pressure from the actor.

7. Interview with Gordon Gow, *Films and Filming,* February 1979

8. *Richard Attenborough's A Chorus Line* (1986)

9. Ibid.

10. Hacker and Price, *Take 10, Contemporary British Film Directors*

11. Interview in the *Sunday Telegraph*, August 1965

12. Richard Attenborough, *In Search of Gandhi,* (London: The Bodley Head, 1982)

13. Ibid.

14. Ibid.

15. In *Answers*, 2 July 1949

16. Interview with Gordon Gow, *Films and Filming*, February 1979

17. Attenborough, *In Search of Gandhi*

18. Ibid.

19. Ibid.

20. Interview with Gordon Gow, *Films and Filming,* February 1979

21. Attenborough, *In Search of Gandhi*

22. Interview in *American Film*

23. Philip French, *Sight and Sound,* Spring 1969

24. Carl Foreman, interview with Ann Guerin, *Show*, December 1972

25. William Goldman, *Adventures in the Screen Trade* (London: Abacus, 1983)

26. Ibid.

27. Ibid.

28. Ibid.

29. Interview with Gordon Gow, *Films and Filming,* February 1979

30. Ibid.

31. Ibid.

32. Ibid.

33. Ibid.

34. Ibid

35. In *The Statesman,* Calcutta, quoted David Castell, *Richard Attenborough* (London: Bodley Head, 1984).

36. Attenborough, *In Search of Gandhi*

37. Interview in the *Sunday Times*

38. Richard Attenborough in Foreword to Donald Woods, *Filming With Attenborough: The Making of Cry Freedom* (New York, 1987)

39. Donald Woods, *Filming With Attenborough*

40. The title, suggested by the co-producer Norman Spencer, only came at a late stage of production. Before that, the working title was *Biko/Asking for Trouble*

41. Woods, *Filming With Attenborough*

42. Richard Attenborough, *Cry Freedom: A Pictorial Record* (London, 1986)

43. Woods, *Filming With Attenborough*

44. Ibid.

45. Ibid.

46. Attenborough, *Cry Freedom, A Pictorial Record*

47. The quotations in this and the two succeeding paragraphs are from Attenborough's 'Reflections on a Decade of the British Film Institute', included as an appendix in the original edition (1992) of this book.

48. Diana Hawkins, in interview, 1992

49. Pam Paumier, in interview, 1992

50. *Chicago Sun-Times*, 1 August 1993

51. James Berardinelli website

52. *Sight and Sound*, January 1993, p.42

53. *Sight and Sound*, January 1995, p.49

54. *Sight and Sound*, March 1997, p.50

CHRONOLOGY

(Titles of stage plays are in italic; titles of films directed by RA are in upper-case bold; other film titles are in upper-case roman.)

1923   29 August. Born Cambridge, England, son of Frederick L. and Mary (née Clegg) Attenborough

1934–41 Wyggeston Grammar School, Leicester

1935   First impresarial enterprise, producing concert in St Barnabas Hall, Leicester

1938–41 Acted as amateur with Leicester Little Theatre

1941   Leverhulme Scholarship to Royal Academy of Dramatic Art (Bancroft Medal)

Ah, Wilderness! (Intimate Theatre, Palmers Green)

Al Parker became RA's agent

1942   *Awake and Sing* (Arts Theatre)

Twelfth Night (Arts Theatre)

London W.1. (Q Theatre)

The Little Foxes (Piccadilly Theatre)

The Holy Isle (Arts Theatre)

Maria Marten, or the Murder in the Red Barn (Arts Theatre)

IN WHICH WE SERVE

1943   SCHWEIK'S NEW ADVENTURES

Brighton Rock (Garrick Theatre)

Joined RAF

1944   THE HUNDRED POUND WINDOW

Seconded to RAF Film Unit

1945   JOURNEY TOGETHER

22 January. Married Sheila Beryl Sim

1946   A MATTER OF LIFE AND DEATH

Demobilised from RAF

SCHOOL FOR SECRETS

1947   THE MAN WITHIN

DANCING WITH CRIME

BRIGHTON ROCK

1948   LONDON BELONGS TO ME

THE GUINEA PIG

THE LOST PEOPLE

1949   BOYS IN BROWN

The Way Back (*Home of the Brave*) (Westminster Theatre)

Sept. Moved home from Chelsea to Old Friars, Richmond

1949–73 Member British Actors Equity Association (Council member 1949–79)

1950   *To Dorothy a Son* (Savoy Theatre, transferred to Garrick Theatre, 1951).

13 February. Birth of son, Michael John Attenborough

Presented radio programme 'Record Rendezvous', introducing such numbers as 'Music, music, music'. There was public indignation when the BBC axed the programme on account of official limitations on 'needle time'.

MORNING DEPARTURE

1951   HELL IS SOLD OUT

1951   THE MAGIC BOX
1952   THE GIFT HORSE
        FATHER'S DOING FINE
        Sweet Madness (Vaudeville Theatre)
1952–4 *The Mousetrap* (Ambassadors Theatre)
1954   EIGHT O'CLOCK WALK
1955   THE SHIP THAT DIED OF SHAME
        3 August. Spoke 'Peter and the Wolf' in a
        performance at the Proms, conducted
        by Sir Malcolm Sargent
        30 September. Birth of daughter, Jane
        Attenborough
1956   PRIVATE'S PROGRESS
        THE SHIP THAT DIED OF SHAME
        Beginning of friendship and collaboration
        with Bryan Forbes
        TALK OF MANY THINGS (TV)
1956–7 *Double Image* (Savoy Theatre; transferred
        to St James Theatre, 1957)
1956–88 Chairman, Actors' Charitable Trust
        (President, 1988–)
1957   BROTHERS IN LAW
        THE SCAMP
1957–8 *The Rape of the Belt* (Piccadilly Theatre)
1958   DUNKIRK
        THE MAN UPSTAIRS
        SEA OF SAND
1959   DANGER WITHIN
        I'M ALL RIGHT JACK
        JET STORM
        S.O.S. PACIFIC
        29 June. Birth of daughter, Charlotte
        Attenborough
        Formed Beaver Films with Bryan Forbes

1960   Formed Allied Film Makers with Bryan
        Forbes, Guy Green, Michael Relph,
        Basil Dearden and Jack Hawkins
        THE ANGRY SILENCE (also co-
        produced)
        THE LEAGUE OF GENTLEMEN
        THEY MADE HISTORY (TV)
1961   ONLY TWO CAN PLAY
        ALL NIGHT LONG
        WHISTLE DOWN THE WIND
        (produced only)
1962   THE DOCK BRIEF
        THE L-SHAPED ROOM (co-produced
        only)
1963   THE GREAT ESCAPE
1963–71 Vice-President, Muscular Dystrophy
        Group of Great Britain (President,
        1971–)
1963–   Member of Council, Royal Academy of
        Dramatic Art
1964   THE THIRD SECRET
        SEANCE ON A WET AFTERNOON
        (also produced)
        Best Actor, San Sebastian Film Festival
        Best Actor, British Film Academy
        GUNS AT BATASI
        Best Actor, British Film Academy
1964–88 Chairman, Combined Theatrical
        Charities Appeals Council (President,
        1988–)
1966   FLIGHT OF THE PHOENIX
1967   **OH! WHAT A LOVELY WAR**
        (co-produced and directed).
        16 international awards including
        Golden Globe, Society of Film and
        Television Arts Award, UN Award

1967   THE SAND PEBBLES. Golden Globe
            Award
            DR DOLITTLE. Golden Globe Award
            Created C.B.E.

1967–73   Cinematograph Films Council

1968   THE BLISS OF MRS BLOSSOM
            ONLY WHEN I LARF

1969   THE MAGIC CHRISTIAN
            DAVID COPPERFIELD

1969–70   Chairman, British Academy of Film and
            Television Arts (formerly SFTA)

1969–82   Director, Chelsea Football Club

1969–90   Patron, Gardner Centre for the Arts,
            Sussex University (President, 1990–)

1970   THE LAST GRENADE
            A SEVERED HEAD
            LOOT
            TEN RILLINGTON PLACE
            Hon. D.LL Leicester University

1970–
2002   Chairman, Royal Academy of Dramatic
            Art

1970–   Pro-Chancellor, Sussex University

1970–81   Governor, National Film School

1970–73   Member of Arts Council of Great Britain

1971   Vice-President, BAFTA

1972   YOUNG WINSTON (produced and
            directed). Golden Globe Award

1973   Chairman of Capital Radio

1974   AND THEN THERE WERE NONE
            ROSEBUD
            Hon. DCL , Newcastle University

1974–84   Director, Young Vic Board

1975   BRANNIGAN
            CONDUCT UNBECOMING
            Trustee, Help a London Child

1976   Created Knight
            Chairman UK Trustees Waterford-
            Kamhlaba School, Swaziland
            (Governor, 1987–)

1976–82   Trustee, Tate Gallery

1977   Governor, Motability
            THE CHESS PLAYERS
            A BRIDGE TOO FAR (directed).
            Evening Standard Best Drama Award

1978   MAGIC (directed)

1979   THE HUMAN FACTOR

1979–   Chairman, Duke of York's Theatre

1979–   Vice-President, SCF

1980–86   Deputy Chairman, Channel Four
            Television (Chairman 1986–1992)

1981   Hon. D.LL Kent University

1981–92   Chairman and Governor, British Film
            Institute.

1982   GANDHI (produced and directed).
            Awarded 5 Golden Globes, 8 Academy
            Awards, 5 BAFTA Awards, Manila
            International Film Festival Golden
            Eagle, Directors' Guild of America
            Award for outstanding directorial
            achievement
            Published *In Search of Gandhi*
            Patron, Kingsley Hall Community Centre

1982-87   Chairman, Goldcrest Films and TV
            Limited

1983   Fellow, BAFTA
            Evening Standard Film Award, for
            Service to British Cinema 1943–83
            Martin Luther King Jr. Peace Prize
            Padhma Bushan, India
            Hon. D.Litt, Dickinson, Penn.
            President, The Gandhi Foundation

1983–5   Chairman, Committee of Inquiry into the
        Arts and Disabled People

1984   President, Brighton Festival

1984–6 President, British Film Year

1985   **A CHORUS LINE** (directed)
        Commandeur, Ordre des Arts et Lettres

1986   Published *Richard Attenborough's A*
        Chorus Line (with Diana Hawkins)
        Trustee, Tate Foundation

1987   **CRY FREEDOM** (produced and
        directed)
        Published *Richard Attenborough's Cry*
        Freedom
        Governor, Waterford-Kamhlaba School,
        Swaziland
        Chair, British Screen Advisory Council
        Goodwill Ambassador for UNICEF
        Hon. D.LL Sussex University

1987–92 Chairman, Channel Four Television

1988   Chairman, European Script Fund
        European Film Awards, Award of Merit
        for Humanitarianism in Film Making

1988–   President, Actors' Charitable Trust

1988–   President, Combined Theatrical Charities
        Appeals

1989   Fleming Memorial Lecture, R.T.S.
        President, Arts for Health

1990   Freeman, City of Leicester
        Patron, Richard Attenborough Centre for
        Disability and the Arts, Leicester

1990   President, Gardner Centre for the Arts,
        Sussex University

1991   Trustee, Foundation for Sport and the
        Arts

1992   Shakespeare Prize for Outstanding
        Contribution to European Culture

1992   **CHAPLIN** (co-produced and directed)
        Life President, Capital Radio
        Patron, The Donkey Sanctuary
        Chairman, Prison Charity Shop Trust
        Takes part in 'Gielgud Looks Back'
        (Channel 4 TV)

1993   Life Peerage in Queen's Honours List
        (12 June), as Lord Attenborough of
        Kingston upon Thames
        SHADOWLANDS (co-produced and
        directed)
        JURASSIC PARK (actor)
        MIRACLE ON 34TH STREET (actor)
        President, Leicester's City Challenge
        Special Award, Variety Club Show
        Business Awards
        Patron, Lloyds Bank Film Challenge
        Patron, Salon Cinema Trust
        Patron, Haymarket Theatre, Basingstoke
        Elected 'Presentation Fellow', King's
        College, London
        South Bank Show's TV Tribute to 70th
        birthday (28 August)
        Richard Attenborough Centre for
        Disability and the Arts awarded grant
        from Foundation for Sports and the Arts

1994   Trustee, Tate Gallery
        Chairman, Criterion Productions
        BAFTA Special Award
        Honorary Fellowship, Manchester
        Metropolitan University
        Attenborough Trust launched by Channel
        4 and British Film Institute
        Honorary Life Membership of Diaspora
        Museum, Tel Aviv
        President, Leicester Bach Choir

1994	Maiden Speech in House of Lords (23 November)	1998	Trustee of Mousetrap Foundation
	Hon. Degree from American International University		Advisory Board of The Roundhouse
			Honorary Patron, with David Attenborough, Leicester Museum 150th anniversary celebrations
1995	RA and Sheila Sim celebrate Golden Wedding anniversary (January)		Praemium Imperiale awarded by Japan Art Association
	ALFS 'Dilys Powell' Award		NPI Hall of Fame Help the Aged Award
	Patron of Guild of Leicester Freemen		Richard and David Attenborough included in Leicester's Ten Most Famous Sons
	Cinema Expo Lifetime Achievement Award		
	Visiting Professor St Catharine's College		
	As Chairman, launches Cinema 100	1999	JOSEPH AND THE AMAZING TECHNICOLOR DREAMCOAT (actor)
	Richard Attenborough Centre receives Arts Council grant of £730,000		
1996	HAMLET (actor)		**GREY OWL** (co-produced and directed)
	E=MC2 (actor)		
	Reported to be preparing film *The Sailmaker*		BAFTA Life Achievement Award
	IN LOVE AND WAR (co-produced and directed)	2000	THE RAILWAY CHILDREN, TV (actor)
	Member of Labour Party's Election Fund Committee		Preparing film about Empress Elisabeth (Sissi) of Austria
1997	THE LOST WORLD: JURASSIC PARK (actor)		Chairman, Board of Old Vic Productions
	Campaigns for Labour Party		Patron of Anne Frank Exhibition
	Trustee, Foundation for Sport and Arts		First Patron, London Film Commission
	Honorary Degree, University of Wales	2001	JACK AND THE BEANSTALK: THE REAL STORY TV miniseries (actor)
	Four-part BBC2 broadcast, 'My Life in Film'		Lifetime Achievement Medal, BT EMMA Awards
	Patron, Sargent Concert Hall Trust		Chairman Dragon Project for new film studio complex in Wales
1998	ELIZABETH (actor)		
	TRESPASSER (actor – voice only)	2002	PUCKOON (actor)
	Patron, MediCinema		President of Royal Academy of Dramatic Art
	Included in Brighton's Walk of Fame		
	Chancellor of Sussex University (at the degree ceremony in July he was reported to have shaken 1,500 hands)		

FILMOGRAPHY

FILMS AS ACTOR

In this section, films are listed and dated according to the date of first exhibition, of any kind (censor screening, trade show, etc.), following the practice of Denis Gifford's British Film Catalogue.

Credits given are generally production company (p.c), producer (p), director (d), script (sc), story source and selected players. The players shown do not necessarily follow original billing, but always include the leading players, along with the names of people who are significant either in Attenborough's career or in cinema history. In each case Attenborough's role name is shown.

In Which We Serve   GB   1942

p.c: Two Cities. p: Nöel Coward. d: David Lean and Nöel Coward. sc: Nöel Coward. With Nöel Coward, John Mills, Bernard Miles, Celia Johnson, Kay Walsh, Joyce Carey, Michael Wilding, Penelope Dudley Ward, Daniel Massey.
RA played Stoker

Schweik's New Adventures   GB   1943

(re-issued 1945 as *It Started At Midnight*)
p.c: Eden Films. p: Walter Sors, Edward G. Whiting. d: Karel Lamac. sc: Karel Lamac, Con West, from Karel Lamac. With Lloyd Pearson.
RA played Worker

The Hundred Pound Window   GB   1944

pc: Warner-First National. d: Brian Desmond-Hurst. sc: Abem Finkel, Brock Williams, Rodney Ackland, from Mark Hellinger. With Anne Crawford, David Farrar, Ruby Miller.
RA played Tommy Draper

Journey Together   GB   1945

p.c: RAF Film Unit/RKO. d/sc: John Boulting. Story: Terence Rattigan. With Edward G. Robinson, Bessie Love, Ronald Squire, Jack Watling, David Tomlinson, Hugh Wakefield, John Justin, George Cole.
RA played David Wilton

A Matter of Life and Death   GB   1946

p.c: Archers. p/d/sc:Michael Powell, Emeric Pressburger. With David Niven, Roger Livesey, Raymond Massey, Kim Hunter, Marius Goring, Robert Coote, Robert Atkins, Edwin Max, Abraham Sofaer, Kathleen Byron.
RA played a pilot: his scene was shot during an informal visit to the studio while he was on 72 hours' leave.

School for Secrets   GB   1946

p.c: Two Cities. p: Peter Ustinov, George H. Brown. d/sc: Peter Ustinov. With Ralph Richardson, Raymond Huntley, Marjorie Rhodes, John Laurie, Finlay Currie, David Tomlinson, Michael Hordern, Bill Rowbotham (Bill Owen).
RA played Jack Arnold

The Man Within   **GB**   **1947**

(US title: *The Smugglers*)

p.c: Production Film Service. p/sc: Muriel and Sydney
Box. d:Bernard Knowles. Story from Graham Greene.
With Michael Redgrave, Jean Kent, Joan Greenwood,
Francis L. Sullivan, Felix Aylmer, Ronald Shiner,
Ernest Thesiger, Basil Sydney.

RA played Francis Andrews

Dancing With Crime   **GB**   **1947**

p.c: Coronet-Alliance. p: Sydney Box, James Mason.
d: John Paddy Carstairs. s: Brock Williams. With
Sheila Sim, Barry K. Barnes, Bill Rowbotham (Bill
Owen), Diana Dors.

RA played Ted Peters

Brighton Rock   **GB**   **1947**

p: Roy Boulting. d: John Boulting. sc: Terence
Rattigan, Graham Greene, from book by Graham
Greene. With Hermione Baddeley, William Hartnell,
Carol Marsh, Nigel Stock, Harcourt Williams,
Constance Smith.

RA played Pinkie Brown

London Belongs to Me   **GB**   **1948**

(US title: *Dulcimer Street*)

p.c: IP-Individual. p: Frank Launder, Sidney Gilliat
d: Sidney Gilliat. sc: Sidney Gilliat, J. B. Williams,
from novel by Norman Collins. With Alastair Sim, Fay
Compton, Susan Shaw, Ivy St Helier, Joyce Carey,
Eleanor Summerfield, Gladys Henson, Hugh Griffith,
Henry Edwards.

RA played Percy Boon

The Guinea Pig   **GB**   **1948**

p.c: Pilgrim. p: John Boulting. d: Roy Boulting.
sc: Warren Chetham Strode, Bernard Miles, Roy
Boulting. With Sheila Sim, Bernard Miles, Joan
Hickson, Anthony Newley.

RA played Jack Read

The Lost People   **GB**   **1948**

p.c: Gainsborough. p: Gordon Wellesley. d: Bernard
Knowles. sc: Bridget Boland, Muriel Box, from play
'Cockpit' by Bridget Boland. With Dennis Price, Mai
Zetterling, Siobhan McKenna, William Hartnell, Jill
Balcon.

RA played Jan

Boys in Brown   **GB**   **1949**

p.c: Gainsborough. p: Anthony Darnborough.
d: Montgomery Tully. sc: Reginald Beckwith. With
Jack Warner, Dirk Bogarde, Jimmy Hanley, Thora
Hird, Graham Payn, Michael Medwin, Alfie Bass.

RA played Jackie Knowles

Morning Departure   **GB**   **1950**

p.c: Jay Lewis. p: Leslie Parkin. d: Roy Baker.
sc: William Fairchild, from play by William Fairchild.
With John Mills, Nigel Patrick, Lana Morris, Helen
Cherry, James Hayter, Zena Marshall, George Cole,
Bernard Lee, Kenneth More. RA played Stoker Snipe

Hell is Sold Out   **GB**   **1951**

p.c: Zelstro. p: Raymond Stross. d: Michael Anderson.
sc: Guy Morgan, Moie Charles, from novel by
Maurice Dekobra. With Mai Zetterling, Herbert Lom,
Kathleen Byron, Hermione Baddeley, Zena Marshall,
Nicholas Hannen, Joan Hickson, Laurence Naismith.

RA played Pierre Bonnet

The Magic Box   GB   1951

p.c: Festival. p: Ronald Neame. d: John Boulting. sc: Eric
Ambler, from Claude Allister's biography 'Friese-Greene'.
With all-star cast including Laurence Olivier, Robert
Donat, Michael Redgrave, Sheila Sim, Dennis Price,
Margaret Rutherford, Sybil Thorndike, David
Tomlinson, Joyce Grenfell, Peter Ustinov, Harcourt
Williams, Emlyn Williams.
RA played Jack Carter

The Gift Horse   GB   1952

(US title: *Glory at Sea*)
p.c: Molton. p: George Pitcher. d: Compton Bennett.
sc: William Fairchild, Hugh Hastings, from story by
Ivan Goff, Ben Roberts. With Trevor Howard, Sonny
Tufts, James Donald, Bernard Lee, Dora Bryan, Hugh
Williams, Sidney James, James Kenney.
RA played Dripper Daniels

Father's Doing Fine   GB   1952

p.c: Marble Arch. p: Victor Skutezky. d: Henry Cass.
sc: Anne Burnaby, from play, 'Little Lambs Eat Ivy' by
Nöel Langley. With Heather Thatcher, Nöel Purcell,
Virginia McKenna, Jack Watling, Sidney James.
RA played Dougal

Eight O'clock Walk   GB   1954

p.c: British Aviation. p: George King. d: Lance
Comfort. sc: Guy Morgan, Katherine Strueby, from
story by Jack Roffey, Gordon Harbord. With Cathy
O'Donnell, Derek Farr, Ian Hunter.
RA played Tom Manning

The Ship That Died of Shame   GB   1955

(US title: *PT Raiders*)
p.c: Ealing. p: Michael Relph. d: Basil Dearden. sc:

Michael Relph, Basil Dearden, John Whiting, from
novel by Nicholas Montserrat. With George Baker,
Bill Owen, Virginia McKenna, Roland Culver, Bernard
Lee, John Longden.
RA played George Hoskins

Private's Progress   GB   1956

p.c: Charter. p: Roy Boulting. d: John Boulting. sc:
John Boulting, Frank Harvey, from novel by Alan
Hackney. With Dennis Price, Terry-Thomas, Ian
Carmichael, Peter Jones, William Hartnell, Ian
Bannen, Miles Malleson, John le Mesurier.
RA played Cox

The Baby and the Battleship   GB   1956

p.c: Jay Lewis. p: Anthony Darnborough. d: Jay Lewis.
sc: Jay Lewis, Gilbert Hackforth-Jones, Bryan Forbes,
from novel by Anthony Thorne. With John Mills,
Andre Morell, Bryan Forbes, Lisa Gastoni, Michael
Hordern, Lionel Jeffries, Thorley Walters, John le
Mesurier, Gordon Jackson.
RA played Knocker White

Brothers in Law   GB   1957

p.c: Tudor. p: John Boulting. d: Roy Boulting.
sc: Roy Boulting, Frank Harvey, Jeffrey Dell, from novel
by Henry Cecil. With Ian Carmichael, Terry-Thomas, Jill
Adams, Miles Malleson, Raymond Huntley, Eric Barker,
Nicholas Parsons, John le Mesurier, Irene Handl.
RA played Henry Marshall

The Scamp   GB   1957

p.c: Lawrie. p: James H. Lawrie. d/sc: Wolf Rilla, from
play by Charlotte Hastings. With Terence Morgan,
Colin Petersen, Dorothy Alison, Jill Adams.
RA played Stephen Leigh

Dunkirk									**GB**		**1958**

p.c: Ealing. p: Michael Forlong. d: Leslie Norman.
sc: W. P. Lipscomb, David Divine, from novel 'The Big
Pickup' by Elleston Trevor. With John Mills, Bernard
Lee, Robert Urquhart, Maxine Audley, Lionel Jeffries.
RA played John Holden

The Man Upstairs								**GB**		**1958**

p.c: ACT Films. p: Robert Dunbar. d: Don Chaffey.
sc: Robert Dunbar, Don Chaffey, from story by Alun
Falconer. With Bernard Lee, Donald Houston,
Dorothy Alison, Virginia Maskell.
RA played Peter Watson

Sea of Sand								**GB**		**1958**

p.c: Tempean. p: Robert Baker, Monty Berman.
d: Guy Green. sc: Robert Westerby, from story by
Sean Fielding. With John Gregson, Michael Craig,
Andrew Faulds, Ray McAnally.
RA played Trooper Brody

Danger Within								**GB**		**1959**

p.c: British Lion. p: Colin Leslie. d: Don Chaffey.
sc: Bryan Forbes, Frank Harvey, from novel 'Death in
Captivity' by Michael Gilbert. With Richard Todd,
Bernard Lee, Michael Wilding, Dennis Price, Donald
Houston.
RA played Captain 'Bunter' Phillips

I'm All Right Jack							**GB**		**1959**

p.c: Charter. p: Roy Boulting. d: John Boulting.
sc: John Boulting, Frank Harvey, Alan Hackney, from
novel 'Private Life' by Alan Hackney. With Ian
Carmichael, Terry-Thomas, Peter Sellers, Margaret
Rutherford, Dennis Price, Irene Handl, Miles
Malleson, Victor Maddern, John le Mesurier,

Raymond Huntley, Cardew Robinson, Malcolm
Muggerdige.
RA played Sidney de Vere Cox

Jet Storm									**GB**		**1959**

p.c: Pendennis. p: Steven Pallos. d: C. Raker Endfield
(Cy Endfield). sc: Sigmund Miller, C. Raker Endfield,
from story by Sigmund Miller. With Stanley Baker,
Diane Cilento, Virginia Maskell, Marty Wilde, Mai
Zetterling, Hermione Baddeley, Bernard Braden,
Barbara Kelly, David Kossoff, Harry Secombe,
Elizabeth Sellars, Sybil Thorndike.
RA played Ernest Tilley

S.O.S. Pacific								**GB**		**1959**

p.c: Remfield. p: John Nasht, Patrick Filmer-Sankey.
d: Guy Green. sc: Robert Westerby. With Pier Angeli,
John Gregson, Eva Bartok, Eddie Constantine, Jean
Anderson.
RA played Whitey.

The Angry Silence								**GB**		**1960**

p.c: Beaver. p: Richard Attenborough, Bryan Forbes.
d: Guy Green. sc: Bryan Forbes, from story by
Michael Craig, Richard Gregson. With Pier Angeli,
Michael Craig, Bernard Lee, Geoffrey Keen, Laurence
Naismith, Oliver Reed.
RA played Tom Curtis

The League of Gentlemen							**GB**		**1960**

p: Allied Film Makers. p: Michael Relph. d: Basil
Dearden. sc: Bryan Forbes, from novel by John
Boland. With Jack Hawkins, Nigel Patrick, Roger
Livesey, Bryan Forbes, Kieron Moore, Robert Coote.
RA played Edward Lexy

Only Two Can Play   GB   1961

p.c: Vale. p: Frank Launder, Sidney Gilliat. d: Sidney
Gilliat. sc: Bryan Forbes, from novel 'That Uncertain
Feeling', by Sidney Gilliat. With Peter Sellers, Mai
Zetterling, Virginia Maskell.

RA played Probert

All Night Long   GB   1961

p.c: Rank. p: Bob Roberts, Michael Relph. d: Basil
Dearden. sc: Nel King, Peter Achilles. With Patrick
McGoohan, Keith Michell, Betsy Blair.

RA played Rod Hamilton

The Dock Brief   GB   1962

p.c: Anatole de Grunwald. p: Dimitri de Grunwald.
d: James Hill. sc: Pierre Rouve, from play by John
Mortimer. With Peter Sellers, Beryl Reid, David
Lodge, Frank Pettingell.

RA played Fowle

The Great Escape   USA/West Germany 1963

p.c: Mirisch/Alpha. p/d: John Sturges. sc: James
Clavell, W. R. Burnett, from book by Paul Brickhill.
With Steve McQueen, James Garner, James Donald,
Charles Bronson, Donald Pleasance, James Coburn,
Gordon Jackson, David McCallum.

RA played Bartlett

Seance on a Wet Afternoon   GB   1964

p.c: Allied Film Makers/Beaver. p: Richard
Attenborough, Bryan Forbes. d/sc: Bryan Forbes, from
novel by Mark McShane. With Kim Stanley, Nanette
Newman, Patrick Magee, Gerald Sim.

RA played Billy Savage

Best Actor, San Sebastian Film Festival

Best Actor, British Film Academy Awards

The Third Secret   GB   1964

p.c: Hubris. p: Robert L. Joseph, Shirley Bernstein.
d: Charles Crichton. sc: Robert L. Joseph. With
Stephen Boyd, Jack Hawkins, Diane Cilento, Pamela
Franklin, Paul Rogers, Alan Webb, Rachel Kempson,
Peter Sallis, Patience Collier, Freda Jackson, Judi
Dench, Nigel Davenport.

RA played Alfred Price-Gorham

Guns at Batasi   GB   1964

p.c: 20th Century-Fox. p: George Brown. d: John
Guillermin. sc: Robert Holles, Leo Marks, Marshall
Pugh, C. M. Pennington-Richards, from novel 'Siege
of Battersea' by Robert Holles. With Flora Robson,
John Leyton, Jack Hawkins, Mia Farrow, Cecil Parker,
Earl Cameron.

RA played R.S.M. Lauderdale

Best Actor, British Film Academy Awards.

Flight of the Phoenix   USA   1966

p.c: TCF Associates and Aldrich. p/d: Robert Aldrich.
sc: Lukas Heller, from novel by Elleston Trevor. With
James Stewart, Peter Finch, Hardy Kruger, Ernest
Borgnine, Ian Bannen, Ronald Fraser, Christian
Marquand, Dan Duryea, George Kennedy.

RA played Lew Moran

The Sand Pebbles   USA   1967

p.c: TCF/Argyle/Solar. p/d: Robert Wise. sc: Robert
Anderson, from novel by Richard McKenna. With
Steve McQueen, Richard Crenna, Candice Bergen,
Marayat Andriane.

RA played Frenchy

Golden Globe Award

Doctor Dolittle   USA   1967

p.c: TCF/APJAC. p: Arthur P. Jacobs. d: Richard
Fleischer. sc: Leslie Bricusse, from the 'Dr Dolittle'
stories by Hugh Lofting. With Rex Harrison,
Samantha Eggar, Anthony Newley.
RA played Albert Blossom
Golden Globe Award

The Bliss of Mrs Blossom   GB   1968

p.c: Paramount. p: Josef Shaftel. d: Joe McGrath. sc:
Alec Coppel, Denis Norden, from play by Alec
Coppel. With Shirley Maclaine, James Booth, Freddie
Jones, Barrie Humphries.
RA played Robert Blossom

Only When I Larf   GB   1968

p.c: Beecord. p: Len Deighton, Brian Duffy. d: Basil
Dearden. sc: John Salmon, from novel by Len
Deighton. With David Hemmings, Alexandra Stewart,
Nicholas Pennell, Melissa Stribling.
RA played Silas

The Magic Christian   GB   1969

p.c: Grand. p: Henry Weinstein, Anthony Unger. d:
Joseph McGrath. sc: Terry Southern, Joseph
McGrath, Peter Sellers, Graham Chapman, John
Cleese. With Peter Sellers, Ringo Starr, Laurence
Harvey, Christopher Lee, Spike Milligan, Yul Brynner,
Roman Polanski, Raquel Welch, Isabel Jeans, Wilfrid
Hyde White, Fred Emney, Hattie Jaques, John le
Mesurier, Dennis Price.
RA played Coach.

David Copperfield   GB   1969

p.c: Omnibus. p: Frederick H. Brogger. d: Delbert
Mann. sc: Jack Pullman, from novel by Charles
Dickens. With Cyril Cusack, Edith Evans, Pamela
Franklin, Susan Hampshire, Wendy Hiller, Ron
Moody, Laurence Olivier, Robin Phillips, Michael
Redgrave, Ralph Richardson, Emlyn Williams, James
Donald, James Hayter, Megs Jenkins, Anna Massey.
RA played Mr Tungay

The Last Grenade   GB   1970

p.c: Lockmore/Cinerama/de Grunwald. p: Josef
Shaftel. d: Gordon Flemyng. sc: Kenneth Ware, James
Mitchell, John Sherlock, from novel 'The Ordeal of
Major Grigsby', by John Sherlock. With Stanley
Baker, Alex Cord, Honor Blackman, John Thaw.
RA played General Charles Whiteley

A Severed Head   GB   1970

p.c: Wincast. p: Alan Ladd Jr. d: Dick Clement. sc:
Frederic Raphael from novel by Iris Murdoch, play,
Iris Murdoch, J. B. Priestley. With Lee Remick, Ian
Holm, Claire Bloom.
RA played Palmer Anderson

Loot   GB   1970

p.c: Performing Arts. p: Arthur Lewis. d: Silvio
Narizzano. sc: Ray Galton, Alan Simpson, from play
by Joe Orton. With Lee Remick, Hywel Bennett, Milo
O'Shea, Roy Holder, Dick Emery.
RA played Truscott

10 Rillington Place   GB   1970

p.c: Genesis/Filmways/Columbia. p: Martin
Ransohoff, Leslie Linder. d: Richard Fleischer. sc:
Clive Exton, from book by Ludovic Kennedy. With
Judy Geeson, John Hurt, Pat Heywood, Robert
Hardy, Andre Morell, Bernard Lee.
RA played John Reginald Christie

And Then There Were None   **GB**   **1974**
p.c: Filibuster Films. p: Harry Alan Towers. d: Peter
Collinson. sc: Peter Welbeck (Harry Alan Towers),
from play 'Ten Little Niggers' by Agatha Christie.
With Oliver Reed, Elke Sommer, Gert Froebe,
Stephane Audran, Charles Aznavour, Herbert Lom,
Orson Welles.
RA played Judge Cannon

Rosebud   **USA**   **1974**
p.c: United Artists. p/d: Otto Preminger. sc: Erik Lee
Preminger, from novel by Joan Hemingway, Paul
Bonnecarrere. With Peter O'Toole, Cliff Gorman,
Claude Dauphin, Peter Lawford, Raf Vallone,
Adrienne Corri.
RA played Sloat

Brannigan   **GB**   **1975**
p.c: Wellborn, for United Artists. p: Jules Levy, Arthur
Gardner. d: Douglas Hickox. sc: Christopher Trumbo,
Michael Butler, William P. McGivern, William Norton.
With John Wayne, Judy Geeson, Mel Ferrer, John
Vernon, John Stride, James Booth, Lesley Ann Down,
Ralph Meeker.
RA played Commander Sir Charles Swann

Conduct Unbecoming   **GB**   **1975**
p.c: Lion International/Crown Production Company.
p: Michael Deeley, Barry Spikings. d:Michael
Anderson. sc: Robert Enders, from play by Barry
England. With Michael York, Trevor Howard, Stacy
Keach, Christopher Plummer, Susannah York.
RA played Major Lionel Roach

The Chess Players   **India**   **1977**
(Shatranj ke Khilari)

p.c: Devri Chitra Productions. p: Suresh Jindal
d/sc: Satyajit Ray, from story by Munshi Premchand.
With Sanjeev Kumar, Saeed Jaffrey, Amjad Khan,
Shabana Azmi. RA played General Outram

The Human Factor   **GB/USA**   **1979**
p.c: Wheel (London)/Sigma (New York). p/d: Otto
Preminger. sc: Tom Stoppard, from novel by Graham
Greene. With Nicol Williamson, Joop Doderer, John
Gielgud, Derek Jacobi, Robert Morley, Ann Todd,
Richard Vernon.
RA played Colonel John Daintry

Jurassic Park   **USA**   **1993**
p.c: Universal/Amblin Entertainment. p: Kathleen
Kennedy, Gerald R. Molen. d: Steven Spielberg.
sc: David Koep, from book by Michael Crichton With
Sam Neill, Laura Dern, Jeff Goldblum, Bob Peck,
Martin Ferrero, B. D. Wong, Joseph Mazzello, Ariana
Richards, Samuel L. Jackson, Wayne Knight, Jerry
Molen.
RA played John Hammond

Miracle on 34th Street   **USA**   **1993**
p.c: 20th Century-Fox. p: John Hughes. d: Les
Mayfield. sc: George Seaton, John Hughes, based on
the 1947 screenplay by George Seaton. With
Elizabeth Perkins, Dylan McDermott, J. T. Walsh, Joss
Ackland.
RA played Kriss Kringle/Santa Claus

Hamlet   **GB**   **1996**
p.c: Castle Rock Entertainment/Columbia p: David
Barron d: Kenneth Branagh. With Kenneth Branagh,
Julie Christie, Billy Crystal, Gerard Depardieu,

Charlton Heston, Derek Jacobi, Jack Lemmon, Rufus Sewell, Robin Williams, Kate Winslet, Ian Mcelhinney, Brian Blessed, Richard Briers, Judi Dench, Reece Dinsdale, Ken Dodd, Nicholas Farrell, Ray Fearon, John Gielgud, Rosemary Harris, Michael Maloney, John Mills, Timothy Spall.
RA played the English Ambassador

$E=mc^2$ GB   1996

p.c: $E=mc^2$ Productions Limited. p: Andre Burgess, Benjamin Fry. d/sc: Benjamin Fry. With Dominic West, Nick Marcq, Jeremy Piven, Kelli Williams, Liza Walker, James Villiers, Byrne Piven
RA played The Visitor

The Lost World: Jurassic Park   USA   1997

p.c: Universal/Amblin Entertainment. d: Steven Spielberg. With Jeff Goldblum, Julianne Moore, Peter Postlethwaite, Arliss Howard, Vince Vaughn, Vanessa Lee Chester, Peter Stormare, Harvey Jason, Richard Schiff, Thomas F. Duffy, Joseph Mazzello.
RA played John Hammond

Elizabeth   GB   1998

p.c: Polygram/Channel 4/Working Title. p: Alison Owen, Eric Fellner, Tim Bevan. d: Shekhar Kapur. sc: Michael Hirst. With Cate Blanchett, Geoffrey Rush, Christopher Eccleston, Joseph Fiennes, Fanny Ardant, Kathy Burke, Eric Cantona, James Frain, Vincent Cassel, Daniel Craig, John Gielgud.
RA played Sir William Cecil, Lord Burghley

Joseph and the Amazing Technicolor Dreamcoat   UK   1999

p.c: Really Useful Films/Polygram/Universal. p: Andrew Lloyd Webber, Andy Picheta, Austin Shaw, Nigel Wright. d: David Mallet, Steven Pimlott. sc: Tim Rice. With Donny Osmond, Maria Friedman, Joan Collins, Christopher Biggins, Robert Torti, Alex Jennings, Nicholas Colicos, Ian McNeice, Jeff Blumenkrantz, David J. Higgins, Patrick Clancy.
RA played Jacob

The Railway Children (TV)   GB   2000

p.c: Carlton Television p: Charles Elton, Freya Pincent, Jonathan Powell. d: Catherine Morshead. sc: Stephen Nye, from E. Nesbit. With Jenny Agutter, Michael Kitchen, Jemima Rooper, Jack Blumeneau, Clare Thomas, Gregor Fisher, Melanie Clark-Pullen, Valerie Minifie, Georgie Glen, Clive Russell, David Bamber.
RA played The Old Gentleman

Jack and the Beanstalk: The Real Story (TV mini-series)   USA   2001

p.c: Hallmark Entertainment/Jim Henson Productions. p: Martin G. Baker, Peter Coogan. d: Brian Henson. sc: James V. Hart, Brian Henson. With Matthew Modine, Vanessa Redgrave, Mia Sara, Daryl Hannah, Jon Voight, Bill Baretta, Honor Blackman, Jim Carter, James Cordon.
RA played Magog, Arbiter of Justice Great Council of Mac Slec

Puckoon   Ireland/GB/Germany   2002

p.c: Y2K Productions, Medienbeteiligungs und Produktions. p: Rainer Mockert, Brooks Riley, Rod Stoneman. d: Terence Ryan. sc: Terence Ryan, from the novel by Spike Milligan. With Sean Hughes, Elliott Gould, Daragh O'Malley, John Lynch, Griff Rhys-Jones, Nickolas Grace, Milo O'Shea, Freddie Jones.
RA played the Writer-Director

FILMS AS PRODUCER ONLY

Whistle Down the Wind   **GB**   **1961**

p.c: Allied Film Makers/Beaver. p: Richard
Attenborough. d: Bryan Forbes. sc: Keith Waterhouse,
Willis Hall, from novel by Mary Hayley Bell. With
Hayley Mills, Bernard Lee, Alan Bates.

The L-Shaped Room   **GB**   **1962**

p.c: Romulus. p: James Woolf, Richard Attenborough.
d/sc: Bryan Forbes, from novel by Lynne Reid Banks.
With Leslie Caron, Tom Bell, Bernard Lee, Brock
Peters, Cicely Courtneidge, Pat Phoenix, Emlyn
Williams, Avis Bunnage, Nanette Newman, Harry
Locke.

FILMS AS DIRECTOR OR PRODUCER/DIRECTOR

Oh! What a Lovely War   **GB**   **1969**

d: Richard Attenborough. sc: Len Deighton (uncred-
ited). Based on the Joan Littlewood/Theatre
Workshop musical play, adapted from the radio
feature 'The Long, Long Trail', by Charles Chilton.
p.c: Accord/Paramount. p: Brian Duffy, Richard
Attenborough. ass.p: Mack Davidson. p.manager:
John Comfort. ass.d: Claude Watson. ph: Gerry
Turpin. Panavision. col: Technicolor. ed: Kevin
Connor. p.des: Don Ashton. a.d: Harry White.
set.dec: Peter James. sp.effects: Ron Ballanger.
m/m.dir: Alfred Ralston. songs: 'Oh! What a Lovely
War', 'Oh I Do Like to be beside the Seaside',
'Belgium Put the Kibosh on the Kaiser', 'Are We
Downhearted?', 'Your King and Country Need You',
'I'll Make a Man of You', 'We're 'Ere Because We're

'Ere', 'Pack Up Your Troubles', 'Heilige Nacht',
'Christmas Day in the Cookhouse', 'Goodbye',
'Gassed', 'Comrades', 'Hush Here Comes a
Whizzbang', 'There's a Long, Long Trail', 'Rule
Britannia', 'I Don't Want to Be a Soldier',
'Mademoiselle From Armentieres', 'The Moon Shines
Bright on Charlie Chaplin', 'Adieu La Vie', 'They Were
Only Playing Leapfrog', 'Forward Joe Soap's Army',
'We Are Fred Karno's Army', 'When This Lousy War is
Over', 'Whiter than the Whitewash on the Wall', 'I
Want to Go Home', 'The Bells of Hell', 'Never Mind',
'Far From Wipers', 'If You Want the Old Batallion',
'Keep the Home Fires Burning', 'Over There', 'They'll
Never Believe Me'. cost: Anthony Mendleson. choreo:
Eleanor Fazan. titles: Raymond Hawkey. sd: Don
Challis, Brian Holland. sd.rec: Simon Kaye. military
adviser: Major-General Sir Douglas Campbell.
CAST: Ralph Richardson (Sir Edward Grey), Meriel
Forbes (Lady Grey), Wensley Pithey (Archduke Franz
Ferdinand), Ruth Kettlewell (Arch Duchess Sophie),
Ian Holm (President Poincaré), John Gielgud (Count
Berchtold), Kenneth More (Kaiser Wilhelm II), John
Clements (General von Moltke), Paul Daneman (Tsar
Nicholas II), Joe Melia (The Photographer), Jack
Hawkins (Emperor Franz Josef), John Hussey (Soldier
on balcony), Kim Smith (Dickie Smith), Mary
Wimbush (Mary Smith), Paul Shelley (Jack Smith),
Wendy Allnutt (Flo Smith), John Rae (Grandpa
Smith), Kathleen Wileman (Emma Smith, aged 4),
Corin Redgrave (Bertie Smith), Malcolm McFee
(Freddie Smith), Colin Farrell (Harry Smith), Maurice
Roeves (George Smith), Angela Thorne (Betty Smith),
John Mills (Field-Marshal Sir Douglas Haig), Julia
Wright (his secretary), Jean-Pierre Cassell (French
Colonel), Penny Allen (solo chorus girl), Maggie Smith
(music hall star), David Lodge (recruiting sergeant),

Michael Redgrave (General Sir Henry Wilson), Laurence Olivier (Field Marshal Sir John French), Peter Gilmore (Private Burgess), Derek Newark (shooting gallery proprietor), Richard Howard (young soldier at Mons), John Trigger (officer at station), Ron Pember (corporal at station), Juliet Mills (first nurse at station), Nanette Newman (second nurse at station), Susannah York (Eleanor), Dirk Bogarde (Stephen), Norman Jones (1st Scottish soldier), Andrew Robertson (2nd Scottish soldier), Ben Howard (3rd Scottish soldier), Angus Lennie (4th Scottish soldier), Brian Tipping (5th Scottish soldier), Christian Doermer (Fritz), Tony Vogel (German soldier), Paul Hansard (German officer), John Woodnutt (British officer), Tony Thawnton (officer on telephone), Cecil Parker (Sir John), Zeph Gladstone (his chauffeur), Stanley McGeagh (first soldier in gassed trench), Stanley Lebor (second soldier in gassed trench), Robert Flemyng (staff officer in gassed trench), Thorley Walters (1st Staff Officer in ballroom), Norman Shelley (2nd Staff Officer in ballroom), Raymond S. Edwards (3rd Staff Officer in ballroom), Isabel Dean (Sir John French's Lady), Guy Middleton (General Sir William Robertson), Natasha Parry (Sir William Robertson's Lady), Cecilia Darby (Sir Henry Wilson's Lady), Phyllis Calvert (Lady Haig), Freddie Ascott ('Whizzbang' soldier), Edward Fox (1st Aide), Geoffrey Davies (2nd Aide), Christian Thorogood (1st Irish soldier), Paddy Joyce (2nd Irish soldier), John Dunhill (3rd Irish soldier), John Owens (4th Irish soldier), P. G. Stephens (5th Irish Soldier), Vanessa Redgrave (Sylvia Pankhurst), Clifford Mollison (1st heckler), Dorothy Reynolds (2nd heckler), Harry Locke (3rd heckler), George Ghent (4th heckler), Michael Bates (drunken lance corporal), Charles Farrell (policeman), Pia Colombo (estaminet singer), Vincent Ball (Australian soldier), Anthony Ainley (3rd Aide), Gerald Sim (chaplain), Maurice Arthur (soldier singer at church parade), Arthur White (sergeant in dugout), Christopher Cabot (soldier in shell hole), Fannie Carby (1st mill girl), Marianne Stone (2nd mill girl), Christine Noonan (3rd mill girl), Charlotte Attenborough (Emma Smith, aged 8).
12,947ft. 144 mins

Young Winston   GB   1972

d: Richard Attenborough. sc: Carl Foreman, based on 'My Early Life', by Winston Churchill. dist: Columbia-Warner. p.c: Open Road/Hugh French. p: Carl Foreman. assoc.p: Harold Buck. p.sup: Michael Stanley-Evans, Sydney G. Barnsby. p.managers: Albert Becket, Cecil F. Ford. ass.d: William P. Cartlidge. ph: Gerry Turpin. Panavision. Eastman Colour. ed: Kevin Connor. des: Geoffrey Drake, Don Ashton. a.d: John Graysmark, Bill Hutchinson. set dec: Peter James. cost: Anthony Mendleson. sp.effects: Cliff Richardson, Tom Howard, Charles Staffel. m: Alfred Ralston. sd.ed: Jonathan Bates. sd.rec: Simon Kaye. sd.re-rec: Bob Jones, Richard Longford.

CAST: Robert Shaw (Lord Randolph Churchill), Anne Bancroft (Lady Randolph Churchill), Simon Ward (Winston Churchill), Jack Hawkins (Mr Weldon), Ian Holm (George E. Buckle), Anthony Hopkins (David Lloyd George), Patrick Magee (General Bindon Blood), Edward Woodward (Captain Haldane), John Mills (General Kitchener), Peter Cellier (Captain, 35th Sikhs), Ronald Hines (Adjutant, 35th Sikhs), Dino Safeek (Sikh soldier), Raymond Huntley (elderly officer), Russell Lewis (Winston, aged 7), Pat Heywood (Mrs Everest), Laurence Naismith (Lord Salisbury), William Dexter (Arthur Balfour), Basil Dignam (Joseph Chamberlain), Willoughby Gray (Gladstone), Robert

Hardy (prep school headmaster), Edward Burnham
(Labouchere), John Stuart (Peel), Colin Blakely
(Butcher), Nöel Davis (interviewer), Michael Audreson
(Winston, aged 13), Richard Leech (Mr Moore), Clive
Morton (Dr Roose), Robert Flemyng (Dr Buzzard),
Reginald Marsh (Prince of Wales), Jeremy Child
(Austen Chamberlain), Robert Lankesheer (sympa-
thetic M.P.), Jane Seymour (Pamela Plowden),
Dinsdale Landen (Captain Weaver), Julian Holloway
(Captain Baker), Thorley Walters (Major Finn), Patrick
Holt (Colonel Martin), Norman Bird (party chairman),
Gerald Sim (engineer), Ron Pember (fireman), James
Cosmo (officer on train), Andrew Faulds (mounted
Boer), Maurice Roeves (Brockie), Richard Beale and
Nigel Hawthorn (Boer sentries), James Cossins
(Barnsby), John Woodvine (Howard), Norman
Rossington (Dewsnap), George Mikell (field cornet),
Raymond Mason (man in theatre gallery), Brenda
Cowling (Mrs Dewsnap), Pippa Steel (Clementine
Hozier), Norman Gay (Sir Charles Dilke), Robert
Harris (Gully), Sanders Watney (Sir Winston
Churchill).
14,130 ft. 157 mins

A Bridge Too Far   GB   1977

d: Richard Attenborough. sc: William Goldman, based
on the book by Cornelius Ryan. dist: United Artists.
p.c: Joseph E. Levine Presents. p: Joseph P. Levine,
Richard P.L evine. co-p: Michael Stanley-Evans. ass.p:
John Palmer. p.sup: Eric Rattray. p.man: Terence
A. Clegg. Dutch liaison: Cornelius Van Eijk. ass.d:
David Tomlin, Steve Lanning, Roy Button, Peter
Waller, Geoffrey Ryan. ph: Geoffrey Unsworth.
Panavision, Technicolor. aerial ph: Robin Browne.
parachute ph: Dave Waterman, John Partington-
Smith. sp.ph.effects: Wally Veevers. ed: Anthony

Gibbs. p.des: Terence Marsh. a.d: Roy Stannard,
Stuart Craig, Alan Tomkins. set.dec: Peter Howitt.
sp.effects: John Richardson. m./m.dir: John Addison.
cost: Anthony Mendleson. make-up: Tom Smith.
titles: Joe Caroff. sd.rec: Simon Kaye. sd.re-rec: Gerry
Humphreys, Robin O'Donoghue. p.consultant:
Gabriel Katzka. technical adviser: Kathryn Morgan
Ryan. military advisers: Col. J. L.Waddy, Col. Frank
A. Gregg. military consultants: Maj-Gen. J. D. Frost,
Gen. James H. Gavin, Lt-Gen. Sir Brian Horrocks,
Maj-Gen. Robert Urquhart, Brig. J. O. E. Vandeleur.
p.ass: Judy Humphreys, Loretta Ordewer, Dena
Vincent, Sheila Collins. stunt arranger: Alf Joint.
military vehicle co-ordinator: Charles Mann.
armourer: Bill Aylmore. Second Unit: p.man: Richard
Bamber. d: Sidney Hayers ass.d: Bert Batt. ph: Harry
Waxman.
CAST: Dirk Bogarde (Lieut-Gen. Frederick Browning),
James Caan (Staff-Sgt Eddie Dohun), Sean Connery
(Maj-Gen. Robert Urquhart), Edward Fox (Major
General Brian Horrocks), Elliott Gould (Colonel
Bobby Stout), Gene Hackman (Maj-Gen. Stanislaw
Sosabowski), Anthony Hopkins (Lt-Col. John Frost),
Hardy Kruger (Maj-Gen. Ludwig), Laurence Olivier
(Dr Spaander), Ryan O'Neal (Brig-Gen. James
A. Gavin), Robert Redford (Maj. Julian Cook),
Maximilian Schell (Lt-Gen. Wilhelm Bittrich), Liv
Ullman (Kate ter Horst), Arthur Hill (Tough Colonel),
Wolfgang Preiss (Field Marshal Gerd von Rundstedt),
Siem Vroom (Underground Leader), Marlies Van
Alcmaer (his wife), Eric Van't Wout (their son), Mary
Smithuysen (old Dutch Lady), Hans Croiset (Hans, her
son), Nicholas Campbell (Capt. Glass), Christopher
Good (Maj. Carlyle), Keith Drinkel (Lt Cornish), Peter
Faber (Capt Harry Bestebreutje), Hans von Borsody
(Capt. Blumentritt), Josephine Peeper (cafe waitress),

Paul Maxwell (Maj-Gen Maxwell Taylor), Walter Kojhut (Field Marshal Model), Hartmut Becker (German sentry), Frank Grimes (Maj. Fuller), Jeremy Kemp (RAF briefing officer), Donald Pickering (Lt-Col. Mackenzie), Donald Douglas (Brigadier Lathbury), Peter Settelen (Lt Cole), Stephen Moore (Major Steele), Michael Byrne (Lt-Col Giles Vandeleur), Paul Copley (Private Wicks), Gerald Sim (Colonel Sims), Harry Ditson (US Private), Erick Chitty (Organist), Brian Hawksley (Vicar), Colin Farrel (Cpl Hancock), Norman Gregory (Private Morgan), Alan Armstrong (Cpl. Davies), Anthony Milner (Private Dodds), Barry McCarthy (Private Clark), Lex van Delden (Private Mathias), Michael Wolf (Model's Aide), Sean Mathias (Irish Guards Lieutenant), Tim Beckman (German Private), Edward Seckerson (British Padre), Tom Van Beek (Jan ter Horst), Bertus Botterman, Henny Alma (Dutch villagers), Ray Jewers (US radio operator), Geoffrey Hinsliff (British wireless operator), Fred Williams (Captain Grabner), John Peel (German Lieutenant), John Judd (Sergeant Clegg), Ben Cross (Trooper Binns), Hilary Minster (British medical officer), David English (Private Andrews), Ben Howard (Sergeant Towns), Michael Graham Cox (Captain Cleminson), Johan Te Slaa, Georgette Reyevski (elderly Dutch couple), Peter Groenier, Adrienne Kleiweg (young Dutch couple), Denholm Elliott (RAF Met. officer), Peter Gordon (US sergeant), Garrick Hagon (Lieutenant Rafferty), Brian Gwaspari (US engineer), Stephen Rayment (Grenadier Guards Lieutenant), Tim Morand (British Corporal), James Wardroper (Private Gibbs), Neil Kennedy (Colonel Barker), John Salthouse (Private 'Ginger' Marsh), Jonathan Hackett (glider pilot), Stanley Lebor (RSM), Jack Galloway (Private Vincent), Milton Cadman (Private Long), David Auker ('Taffy' Brace),

Richard Kane (Colonel Weaver), Toby Salaman (Private Stephenson), Michael Bangerter (British Staff Colonel), Philip Raymond (Grenadier Guards Colonel), Myles Reithermann (boat truck driver), Anthony Pullen (US Captain), John Morton (US Padre), John Ratzenberger (US Lieutenant), Patrick Ryecart (German Lieutenant), Dick Rienstra (Captain Krafft), Ian Liston (Sergeant Whitney), Paul Ratter (Private Gordon), Mark Sheridan (Sergeant Tomblin), George Innes (Sergeant Macdonald), John Stride (Grenadier Guards Major), Niall Padden, Michael Graves (British medical orderlies), Simon Chandler (Private Simmonds), Edward Kalinski (Private Archer), Shaun Curry (Cpl. Robbins), Sebastian Abineri (Sergeant Treadwell), Chris Williams (Corporal Merrick), Andrew Branch (flute player), Anthony Garner (British Staff Major), Feliks Arons (Dutch priest), Stuart Blake, Ray Boyd, Stephen Churchett, Jon Croft, Patrick Dickson, Adrian Gibbs, Jason Gregory, Stewart Guidotti, Patrick Hannaway, Brian Haughton, Anthony Howden, Frank Jarvis, David Killick, Dan Lon, Gerald Martin, Edward McDermott, Tony McHale, Jack McKenzie, Francis Mughan, Richard Ommaney, Peter Quince, Robin Scobey, Farrell Sheridan, James Snell, Michael Stock, David Stockton, Paul Vaughan-Teague, Jason White, Mark York. 15,818 ft. 175 mins

Magic   USA   1978

d: Richard Attenborough. sc: William Goldman, based on his own novel. p.c: Joseph E. Levine Productions. exec.p: C. O. Erickson. p: Joseph E. Levine, Richard P. Levine. p.co-ordinator: Joy Anzarouth. p.manager: C. O. Erickson, Alex Hapsas. location co-ordinator (New York): Murray Miller. ass.d: Arne Schmidt, Jerald Sobul, (New York) Mike Haley, François

Moullin. ph: Victor J. Kemper. col: Technicolor. Prints by DeLuxe. ed: John Bloom. ass.ed: Douglas Robertson. p.des: Terence Marsh. a.d: Richard Lawrence. set dec: John Franco Jnr. sp.effects: Robert MacDonald Jnr. m: Jerry Goldsmith. cost: Ruth Myers. make-up: Lee Harman, Hallie Smith-Simmonns, (New York) Robert Laden. sd.ed: Jonathan Bates. sd.rec: Larry Jost, (New York) John Bolz. sd.re-rec: Gerry Humphreys. ventriloquism consultant: Dennis Alwood. magic consultants: Michael Bailey, Lewis Horwitz. dialect adviser: Patrick Watkins. accent consultant: Robert Easton.

CAST: Anthony Hopkins (Corky Withers), Ann-Margret (Peggy Ann Snow), Burgess Meredith (Ben Greene), Ed Lauter (Duke), E. J. Andre (Merlin), Jerry Houser (Cab Driver), David Ogden Stiers (Todson), Lillian Randolph (Sadie), Joe Lowry (Club MC), Beverly Sanders (Laughing Lady), I. W. Klein (Maitre D'), Stephen Hart (Captain), Patrick McCullough (Doorman), Bob Hackman (Father), Mary Munday (Mother), Scott Garrett (Corky's brother), Brad Beesley (Young Corky), Michael Harte (Minister).

9,634 ft. 107 mins

Gandhi   GB   1982

d: Richard Attenborough. sc: John Briley.
dist: Columbia-EMI-Warner. p.c: Indo-British Films, in association with International Film Investors, Goldcrest Films International, National Film Development Corporation of India. exec.p: Michael Stanley-Evans. p: Richard Attenborough. co-p: Rani Dube. assoc.p: Suresh Jindal. p.sup: Terence A.Clegg. p.co-ord: Loretta Ordewer. p.managers: Alexander de Grunwald, Shama Habibullah. loc.man: Graham Ford, Sudesh Sayal. unit mans: Grani O'Shannon,

Gerry Levy, Rashid Abbasi. post-p.ass: Margaret Adams. ass.d: David Tomblin, Steve Lanning, Roy Button, Peter Waller, Kamal Swaroop, M. Shahjehan, Bhisham Bhasin, Julian Wall. ph: Billy Williams, Ronnie Taylor. Panavision. Technicolor. cam.op: Chic Anstiss. aerial ph: Robin Browne. ed: John Bloom. assembly ed: Chris Ridsdale. assoc.ed: Alan Patillo. des: Stuart Craig. a.d: Bob Laing (sup), Ram Yedekar, Norman Dorme. set dec: Michael Seirton. set dressers: Jill Quertier, Nissar Allana, Amal Allana, Aruna Harprasad. costumes: John Mollo, Bhanu Athiya. Indian cost: Manju Raj Saraogi. wardrobe: Nicholas Ede. Indian wardrobe adviser: Sina Kaul. sp.effects sup: David Watkins. m: Ravi Shankar. orchestral score, addit.m: George Fenton. m.co-ordinators: Vijay Raghav Rao, Francis Silkstone. m.perf.by: Vijay Raghav Rao, Sultan Khan, Sharad Khumar, T. K. Ramakrishnan, Lakshmi Shankar, Ashish Khan, Ashit Desai, P. Desai, members of the Wren Orchestra. m.d: George Fenton. make-up: Tom Smith. titles: Advance Film Promotions. sd.ed: Jonathan Bates. sd.rec: Simon Kaye, (m) John Richards. Dolby stereo. sd.re-rec: Gerry Humphreys, Robin O'Donoghue. historical consultant: Professor R. Puri. military adviser: Colonel Blachandra. research: Lorna Mueller. p.ass: Sharlene Chatelier, Eleanor Chaudhuri. stunt co-ord: Gerry Crampton. 2nd unit: p.manager: Devi Dutt. loc.man: Rajiv Suri. d/ph: Govind Nihalani. ass.d: U. S. Pani, John Matthew. cam.op: A. K. Bir.

CAST: Ben Kingsley (Mahatma Gandhi), Candice Bergen (Margaret Bourke-White), Edward Fox (General Dyer), John Gielgud (Lord Irwin), Trevor Howard (Judge Broomfield), John Mills (The Viceroy), Martin Sheen (Walker), Ian Charleson (Charlie Andrews), Athol Fugard (General Smuts), Gunter

Maria Halmer (Herman Kallenbach), Geraldine James (Mirabehn), Amrish Puri (Khan), Saeed Jaffrey (Sardar Patel), Alyque Padamsee (Mohammed Ali Jinnah), Roshan Seth (Pandit Nehru), Rohini Hattangadi (Kasturba Gandhi), Ian Bannen (senior police officer), Michael Bryan (principal secretary), Richard Griffiths (Collins), Bernard Hepton (GOC), Shreeram Lagoo (Professor Gokhale), Virendra Razdan (Maulana Azad), John Clements (Advocate General), Nigel Hawthorn (Kinnoch), Michael Hordern (Sir George Hodge), Om Puri (Nahari), Richard Veron (Sir Edward Gait), Harsh Nayyar (Nathuram Godse), Prabhakar Patankar (Prakash), Vijay Kashyap (Akte), Nigam Prakash (Kakare), Supriya Pathak (Manu), Nina Gupta (Abha), Shane Rimmer (commentator), Peter Harlowe (Lord Mountbatten), Anang Desai (J. B. Kripalani), Winston Ntshona (porter), Peter Cartwright (European passenger), Marius Weyers (conductor), Richard Mayes (Baker), Alok Nath (Tyeb Mohammed), Dean Gasper (Singh), Ken Hutchison (police sergeant), Norman Chancer (reporter), Gulshan Kapoor (rich merchant), Chlu Bara Chokshi (Ayah), Rai Chaturvedi (Harilal Gandhi), Avpar Jhita (Mnital Gandhi), Anthony Saggar (Ramdas Gandhi), David Gant (Daniels), Daniel Day Lewis (Colin), Ray Burdis (youth), Daniel Peacock (2nd youth), Avis Bunnage (Colin's mother), Caroline Hutchison (Sonia Schlesin), Mohan Agashe (Tyeb Mohammed's friend), Sudhanshu Mushra (man in gallery), Dina Nath (miner), John Savident (mine manager), John Patrick (mounted police sergeant), Michael Godley (clergyman), Stewart Harwood (Prison Officer), Stanley McGeagh (prison guard), Christopher Good (young Englishman), David Markham (older Englishman), Jyoti Sarup (young Indian reporter), John Naylor (English reporter), Winston George (American reporter), Hansu Mehta (older Indian reporter), Sudarshan Sethi (Motilal Nehru), Sunila Pradhan (Mrs Motilal Nehru), Moti Makan and Jalal Agha (travellers on train roof), Rupert Frazer (cavalry troop leader), Manohar Pitakli (Shukla), Homi Daruvala, K. K. Raina, Vivek Swaroop and Raja Biswas (Nehru's friends), Dominic Guard (subaltern), Bernard Hill (Sergeant Putnam), Ram Kant Jha (village leder), Nana Palsikar (villager), Alpna Gupta (villager's wife), Chandrakant Thakkar (policeman), John Quentin (batsman), Graham Seed (wicket keeper), Keith Drinkel (Major), Bob Barbeia (police guard), Gerald Sim (magistrate), Colin Farrell (clerk), Sanjeev Puri (young man), Gareth Forwood (secretary), Vijay Crishna (chauffeur), Sunkalp Dubey (servant), James Cossins (Brigadier), Gurcharan Singh (speaker in Jallianwalla Bagh), John Vine (ADC), Geoffrey Chater (government advocate), Ernest Clark (Lord Hunter), Habib Tanveer (Indian barrister), Pankj Mohan (Mahadev Desai), Subhash Gupta and Aadil (policemen at Chauri Chaura), Rajeshwar Nath and S. S. Thakur (marchers at Chauri Chaura), Rahul Gupta (boy with goat), Barry John (police superintendant), Brian Oulton (clerk of court), James Snell, John Boxer and Gerard Norman (court reporters), Bernard Horsfall (General Edgar), Richard Leech (Brigadier), Pankaj Kapoor (Pyarelal), Tarla Mehta (Sarojini Naidu), David Sibley (Subaltern), Daleep Tahil (Zia), Stanley Lebor (police officer), Terrence Hardiman (Ramsay MacDonald), Monica Gupta (little girl), John Croft (Colonel), William Hoyland (Adjutant), John Ratzenberger (American Lieutenant), Jack McKenzie (Major at Aga Khan palace), Tom Alter (doctor at Aga Khan palace), Jane Myerson (Lady Mountbatten), Roop Kumar Razdan (Hindu youth at Ashram), Bani Sharad Joshi (woman refugee), Vagish Kumar Singh (man refugee), Dilsher Singh (Abdul Ghaffar Khan), Sudheer Dalavi (police Commissioner), Tilak Raj (Tahib), Irpinder Puri (Sushila Nayyar), Pren Kapoor, Vinay Apte, Aswami Kumar, Avinash Dogra, Shreedhar Joshi, Suhash Palsikar (Hindu youths in Calcutta street), Karkirat Singh (Nehru's aide), Sekhar Chatterjee (Suhrawardy), Amarjit, Pratap Desai, Bhatawadekar Prakash, Sunil Shende and Rovil Sinnha (Goondas).

16,958 ft. (35mm)/21,056 ft. (70mm). 188 mins

A Chorus Line   USA   1985

d: Richard Attenborough. sc: Arnold Schulman, based on the play by James Kirkwood and Nicholas Dante. p.c: Embassy Films Associates/Polygram Pictures. exec.p: Gordon Stulberg. p: Cy Feuer, Ernest H. Martin. ass.p/unit p.manager: Joseph M. Caracciolo. p.sup: Michael S. Glick. p.office co-ordinator: Jane Raab. location manager: Clayton Townsend. ass.d: Robert Guirolami, Louis D'Esposito, Amy Sayres, James Skotchdopole. ph: Ronnie Taylor. col: Technicolor. add.ph: Richard Kratina, Peter Norman. aerial ph: Don Sweeney. camera op: Thomas Priestley, Jr. Louma crane technician: Stuart Allen. playback op: Neil Fallon. ed: John Bloom. p.des: Patrizia von Brandenstein. a.d: John Dapper. set dec: George DeTitta. set dresser: Marty Rosenberg. mus: Marvin Hamlisch. lyrics: Edward Kleban. m.d./arrangements: Ralph Burns. m.ed: Michael Tronick. m.consultant: Russ Regan (Polygram Records). dance m.layouts: Joseph Joubert, Robert E. Wooten Jr. chor: Jefrey Hornaday. cost.des: Faye Poliakin. cost. consultant: Toyce Anderson. wardrobe sup: Jennifer Nicholas, Bill Christians. make-up: Allen Weisinger. title des: Richard Morrison. titles: Optical Film Effects. sup.sd.ed: Jonathan Bates. sd.rec: Chris Newman, Arthur Bloom,

(mus.) Michael Farrow. Dolby stereo. Dolby engineer: Michael Dicosimo. sd.re-rec: Donald O'Mitchell, Gerry Humphreys, Michael Minkler, Robin O'Donoghue, Kevin O'Connell. audio transfers: (New York) Rick Nicholas. p.ass: John Saffir, Jane Paul, Karen Sloe, Jed Feuer. helicopter pilot: Al Cerullo. CAST: Michael Douglas (Zack), Alyson Reed (Cassie), Terrence Mann (Larry), Michael Blevins (Mark Tabori), Yamil Borges (Diana Morales), Jan Gan Boyd (Connie Wong), Gregg Burge (Richie Walters), Cameron English (Paul), Tony Fields (Al DeLuca), Nicole Fosse (Kristine Erlick), Vicki Frederick (Sheila Bryant), Janet Jones (Judy Monroe), Michelle Johnston (Bebe Benson), Audrey Landers (Val Clark), Pam Klinger (Maggie Winslow), Charles McGowan (Mike Cass), Justin Ross (Greg Gardner), Blane Savage (Don Kerr), Matt West (Bobby Mills), Sharon Brown (Kim), Pat McNamara (Robbie), Sammy Smith (doorman), Timothy Scott (boy with headband), Bambi Jordan (girl in yellow trunks), Richard DeFabees, Melissa Randel, Jeffrey Cornell, Karen Prunczik and Jennifer Kent (reject dancers), Mansoor Najee-Ullah (cab driver), Peter Fitzgerald (dancer with gum), John Hammil (advertising executive), Jack Lehnert (poster-man), Gloria Lynch (taxi passenger), Gregg Huffman (misfit boy dancer), Eric Aaron, Annemarie, Michele Assaf, Buddy Balou, Tina Bellis, Ida Broughton, Brian Bullard, Bill Bushnell, Sergio Cal, Linda Cholodenko, Christine Colby, Anne Connors, Jeffrey Cornell, Frank Cruz, Kim Darwin, John Deluca, Rickee Farrell, Penny Fekany, Angel Ferreira, Ed Forsyth, David Gibson, Darrell Greene, Tonda Hannum, Laura Harman, Sonya Hensley, Linda Hess, Craig Innes, Reed Jones, Barbara Kovac, Andrew Kraus, Michael Lafferty, Barbara Lavorato, Mia Malm, Celia Marta, Liz McLellan, Gwendolyn Miller, Gregory Mitchell, Edd

Morgan, Charles Murray, Arleen Ng, Alan Onickel, Peggy Parten, Helene Phillips, Richard Pierlon, Rhett Pyle, Vicki Regan, Tia Riebling, Debbie Roche, Adrian Rosario, Patricia Ruck, Mark Ruhala, Lynne Savage, Jeanna Schweppe, Jodi Sperduto, Leslie Stevens, William Sutton, Kirby Tepper, Evelyn Tosi, Linda Von Germer, James Walski, Marsha Watkins, Melanie Winter, Lily Lee Wong, Barbara Yeager, Khandi Alexander, David Askler, Bryant Baldwin, Carol Baxter, Robin Brown, Anna Bruno, Cheryl Burr, Roxanna Cabalero, Joe Anthony Cavise, Cheryl Clark, Alexander Cole, Leslie Cook, Alice Cox, Amy Danis, Gary-Michael Davies, Anita Ehrler, Denise Faye, Felix, Scott Fless, William Gabriner, Sandra Gray, Michael Scott Gregory, Niki Harris, D. Michael Heath, Dawn Herbert, Regina Hood, Cindy Lauren Jackson, Bob Keller, Stanley Kramer, Wayde Laboissonniere, Brett Larson, Rodney Allen MaGuire, Monique Mannen, Frank Mastrocola, Nancy Melius, Brad Miskell, Debi A. Monahan, Bob Morrisy, Ron Navarre, Reggie O'Gwyn, Lorent Palacios, Keri Lee Pearsall, Lacy Phillips, Scott Plank, Bubba Dean Rambo, Daryl Richardson, Michael Rivera, Leora Ron, Elissa Rosati, Michelle Rudy, George Russell, Anne Louise Schaut, Kimry Smith, Ty Stephens, Mary Ellen Stuart, Scott Taylor, Christopher Todd, David Vernon, Bobby Walker, Robert Warners, Faruma Williams, Scott Wise, Leslie Woodies (dancers).

13,216 ft. (70mm). 118 mins

Cry Freedom GB 1987

d: Richard Attenborough. sc: John Briley. p.c: Marble Arch Productions for Universal. exec.p: Terence Clegg. p/d: Richard Attenborough. co-p: Norman Spencer, John Briley. p.co-ordinator: Judy Thornton. p.managers: Allan James, Gerry Levy. location manager: Rory Kilalea. casting: Susie Figgis, (Zimbabwe) Andrew Whaley, (crowd) Liz James. ass d: David Tomblin, Steve Chigorimbo, Roy Button, Patrick Kinney, Steve Fillis, Sue Sheldon, Clive Stafford, David Bennett. ph: Ronnie Taylor. Panavision. Colour. cam.op: Eddie Collins. ed: Lesley Walker. p.des: Stuart Craig. a.d: Norman Dorme, George Richardson (sup.), John King. set dec: Michael Seirton. draughtsman: Mike Philllips. sketch artist: Tony Wright. costumes: John Mollo. wardrobe: Kenny Crouch, Lisa Johnson. make-up: Wally Schneiderman, Beryl Lehrman. titles/opticals: Geoff Axtell Associates. sd.ed: Jonathan Bates, (dial.) Brian Mann, Mike Crouch. footsteps ed: Chris Kelly. sd.rec: Simon Kaye. (mus.) Keith Grant (Twickenham Music Studios). Dolby stereo. sd.re-rec: Gerry Humphreys. synthesisers: Ken Freeman. principal consultants: Donald Woods, Wendy Woods, (additional) Mailton Zolile Keke, Majakathata Mokoena. sp.adviser to Richard Attenborough: Dalindlela Tambo. p.ass: Leila Kirkpatrick. stunt co-ordinator: Peter Brace. sp.effects sup: David Harris. sp.effects technicians: Martin Gant (senior), Paul Knowles, Alan Poole, Gift Nyamiandi. m: George Fenton, Jonas Gwangwa. add.orchestrations: Peter Whitehouse.

SECOND UNIT: d: Peter MacDonald. ass.d: Steve Harding, Edwin Angless, Nikolas Korda. ph: Peter MacDonald. cam.op: John Campbell.

CAST: Kevin Kline (Donald Woods), Penelope Wilton (Wendy Woods), Denzel Washington (Steve Biko), John Hargreaves (Bruce), Alec McCowen (Acting High Commissioner), Kevin McNally (Ken), Zakes Moke (Father Kani), Ian Richardson (State Prosecutor), Josette Simon (Dr Ramphele), John Thaw (Kruger), Timothy West (Captain de Wet), Miles Anderson (Lemick), Tommy Buson (Tami), Tim Findley (Peter Jones), Julian Glover (Don Card), Kate

Hardie (Jane Woods), Alton Kumalo (speaker), Louis Mahoney (Lesotho government official), Maw Makondo (Jason), Joseph Marcell (Moses), John Matshikiza (Mapetla), Sophie Mgcina (Evalina), John Paul (Wendy's stepfather), Wabei Siyolwe (Tenjy), Gwen Watford (Wendy's mother), Juanita Waterman (Ntsiki Biko), Graeme Taylor (Dillon Woods), Adam Stuart Walker (Duncan Woods), Hamish Stuart Walker (Gavin Woods), Spring Stuart Walker (Mary Woods), Evelyn Sithole and Xoliswa Sithole (nurses at clinic), James Coine (young boy), Albert Ndinda (Alec), Andrew Whaley (sub-editor), Shelley Borkum (Woods' receptionist), Patricia Gumede (shebeen queen), Angela Gavaza (shebeen queen's niece), Nocebo Mlambo (aunt), Walter Matemavi (nephew), Clement Muchachi (father), Ruth Chinamando (mother), Basil Chidyamathamba (brother-in-law), Marcy Mushore (niece), Lawrence Simbarashe (informer), Carl Chase and Morgan Shepherd (policemen), Tichatonga Mazhindu (Diklima), Neil McPherson (Lemick's assistant), Hepburn Graham (Soga), Claude Maredza (1st rugby player), Carlton Chance (2nd rugby player), Glen Murphy (1st security guard), Russell Keith Grant (2nd security guard), Munyaradzi Kaneventi (Samora Biko), George Lovell (Nkosinathi Biko), Andrew McCulloch (policeman Nel), Graham Fletcher Cook (Nel's partner), Karen Drury (young secretary), Niven Boyd (1st roadblock policeman), Tony Vogel (2nd roadblock policeman), Christopher Hurst (3rd roadblock policeman), Gerald Sim (police doctor), Peter Cartwright (senior police officer), Gary Whelan (police sergeant), Dudley Dickin (nationalist party delegate), David Trevena (mortician), Badi Uzzaman (mortician's assistant), Robert Phillips (speaker at funeral), Fishoo Tembo (Biko's brother), Peggy Marsh (Helen Suzman), Gwyneth Strong (girl at funeral), Philip Bretherton (Major Boshoff), Paul Herzberg (Beukes), Robert MacNamara and Hans Sittig (security policemen), Kimpton Mativenga (black security policeman), David Henry (Afrikaner farmer), Michael Turner (Judge Boshoff), Kalie Hnekom (Magistrate Prins), Paul Jerricho (Sergeant Louw), Star Ncube (1st prisoner), David Guwaza (2nd prisoner), Hilary Minster (1st passport control officer), James Aubrey (2nd passport control officer), Peter Cary (white frontier policeman), Dominic Kanaventi (black frontier policeman), Sam Mathambo (Lesotho passport officer), Walter Muparutsa (Lesotho businessman), Judy Cornwall (receptionist), Michael Graham Cox (3rd passport control officer), John Hartley (4th passport control officer), Simon Shumba (young Lesotho official), Garrick Hagon (McElrea), Nick Tate (Richie), Marilyn Poole (Acting Commissioner's wife), William Marlowe (police Captain at Soweto).

14,193 ft. 158 mins

Chaplin   GB   1992

d: Richard Attenborough. sc: William Boyd and William Goldman. story: Diana Hawkins, based on 'My Autobiography', by Charles Chaplin and 'Chaplin – His Life and Art' by David Robinson.

p.c: Carolco/Le Studio Canal+/RCS Video Production, in association with Japan Satellite Broadcasting, Inc. A Lambeth Production. p: Richard Attenborough, Mario Kassar. assoc.p: Diana Hawkins. co-p: Terence Clegg. ass d: David Tomblin. key 2nd ass.d: Lee Cleary. sc.sup: Nikki Clapp, ph: Sven Nykvist A.S.C. Panavision. Colour. cam.op: Kevin Jewison. ed: Anne V. Coates. p.des: Stuart Craig. sup.a.d: Norman Dorme. storyboard artist: Martin Asbury. m/m.d: John Barry. prod.sd.mixer: Edward Tise. costumes: John Mollo, Ellen Mirojnick. make-up: Wally Schneiderman. Chaplin prosthetic ageing make-up: John Caglione Jr. key make-up: Jill Rockow. hair stylist sup: Stephanie Kaye. tech.adviser: David Robinson. dialect coach: Andrew Jack. Casting: Mike Fenton, Valorie Massalas, Susie Figgis. casting co-ord: Amy Allen Clegg. stills: David James. p.assoc: Alison Webb. financial cont: Jo Gregory. prod.auditor: Marichu Walker.

IN CALIFORNIA (Santa Clarita, Fillmore and locations): unit prod.man: Chris Coles. prod.co-ord: Gina Fortunato. 2nd ass.d: Peter C. Graupner. cam.ass: Jeff Cronenweth, Bob Brown. ass.to Sven Nykvist: Lukacz Bielan. gaffer: 'Aggie' Aguilar. loc.man: Elizabeth Matthews. a.d: Mark Mansbridge. ass.a.d: Geoff Hubbard. set des: Stan Tropp, Don Woodruff. set dec: Chris A. Butler. construction co-ord: Butch West. loc.man: Elizabeth Matthews. prop. master: Larry Bird. props: Ken Zimmerman, Richard Baum, Greg Benge. ass.cost.des: Cynthia Hamilton. cost.sup: Michael Dennison, Deborah Hopper, Anthony Scarano. ass.eds: Jeff Jones, Jim Garrett. hist.adviser: Mark Wanamaker. Chaplin choreog: Dan Kamin. choreog: Susanne McKenrick. sp.effects co-ordinator: Alan E. Lorimer. sp.effects: Paul Stewart, Paul Guest, James Lorimer. stunt co-ord: Joe Dunne. SECOND UNIT (CALIFORNIA). d: Mickey Moore. ass.d: Pat Regan. ph: Alex Witt. loc.man: Diana Myers.

IN LONDON (Pinewood Studios and locations): unit p.man: Basil Somner. 2nd ass.d: Patrick Kinney. loc.mans: Nick Daubeny, Richard Dunmore. a.d: John King. des.ass: Frank Gardiner. set dec: Stephenie McMillan. property master: Peter Hancock. lettering artist: Robert Walker. scenic artist: Brian Bishop. wardrobe: Kenny Crouch, Lisa Johnson. make-up: Pauline Heys, Beryl Lehrman.

sp.effects sup: David Harris. Chaplin choreog: Johnny Hutch. choreog: Kate Platt. stunt co-ord: Peter Brace. fall adviser: Andy Bradford. p.co-ord: Leila Kirkpatrick.

IN VEVEY: unit man: Sandor van Orosz. loc.man: Allan James. stills: Peter Hamshire.

POST-PRODUCTION: Carolco post-prod.sup: Michael Sloan. 1st ass.ed: Christopher Lloyd. 2nd ass.ed: Adrian Trent. sd.ed: Jonathan Bates. ass.sd.ed: Brian Mann. dial.ed: Mike Crouch. ass.dial.ed: David Trent. footsteps ed: Peter Holt. re-rec.mixer: John Bateman. mus.ed: Andrew Glen. ass.mus.ed: Jonathan Enraght-Moony. mus.sd.engineer: Shawn Murphy. orch: Nic Raine.

CAST: Robert Downey Junior (Charles Chaplin), Dan Aykroyd (Mack Sennett), Geraldine Chaplin (Hannah Chaplin), Kevin Dunn (J. Edgar Hoover), Anthony Hopkins (George Haydon), Moira Kelly (Oona O'Neill Chaplin, Hetty Kelly), Kevin Kline (Douglas Fairbanks), Diane Lane (Paulette Goddard), Penelope Ann Miller (Edna Purviance), Paul Rhys (Sydney Chaplin), John Thaw (Fred Karno), Marisa Tomei (Mabel Normand), Nancy Travis (Joan Barry), James Woods (Lawyer Joseph Scott); and (in order of appearance) Hugh Downer (Charles Chaplin, aged 5), Nicholas Gatt (Sydney Chaplin, aged 9), Bill Paterson (stage manager, Aldershot), Anthony Bowles (theatre orchestra conductor, Aldershot), Bryan Coleman (drunk), Howard 'Lew' Lewis, P. H. Moriarty (workhouse officials), Brian Lipson, Alan Ford (warders), Tom Bradford (Charles Chaplin, aged 14), Liz Porter (matchgirl), Ultan Ely-O'Carroll (Rummy Binks), Marcus Eyre (policeman), Anwar Adaoui, Ben Bilson, Matthew Cartwright, Ian Covington, Adam Goodwin, Willy Gregory, Sam Holland, Josh Maguire, Daniel Sherman, Luke Strain, Frankie Sullivan (Lambeth kids), Karen Salt (small girl), Gerald Sim (asylum doctor), Una Brandon-Jones, Audrey Laybourne (asylum inmates), Graham Sinclair (master of ceremonies, provincial music hall), Karen Lewis, Andree Bernard, Carole Jahme, Jacqueline Leonard, Claire Perriam, Theresa Petts (Yankee Doodle Girls), David Gant (Maitre d' at Trocadero), Mary Healey ('Mrs Karno'), Malcolm Terris (coffee stall proprietor), Matthew Cottle (Stan Jefferson), Jade Hykush (hooker in Butte, Montana), Andrzej Borkowski (Polish immigrant), Joseph Alessi (Italian immigrant), Phil Brown (projectionist), Ena Baga (nickelodeon pianist), Mario Govoni (Mario Govoni, Chaplin's butler at Vevey), Dan Kamin (Keystone Kop), David Mooney (photographer in Keystone wedding), C. J. Golden (bride's mother), Raymond Lynch (bride's father), Peter Georges (groom), Mike Randleman (groom's mother), Mike Peluso (groom's father), Caroline Cornell, Ann Fairlie, Paul Hayes, Denis Vero (Keystone wedding guests), Francesca Buller (Minnie Chaplin), Nick Corello (Sennett's masseur), Richard Fast ('Bronco Billy' Anderson), Milla Jovovich (Mildred Harris), Brad Parker (party photographer), Yoshio Be (Kono), Peter Crook (Frank Hooper), David Totheroh (Jack Wilson, second cameraman at Chaplin studio), Jack Totheroh (cameraman at studio opening), Jack Ritschel (William Randolph Hearst), Heather McNair (Marion Davies), Laura Bastianelli, Joy Claussen, Paul Bruno Grenier, Marykate Harris, Charles Howerton, Jason Logan, Renata Scott, Mike Villani (guests at Hearst dinner), Jerry Jenson (hotel porter), Larry Randolph (waiter), Alan Caroff, Daha Craig, Ken Magee (federal marshals), Ben Whitrow (London station master), Edward Crandle (young autograph hunter), Stuart Richman, Mark Vegh (barmen), Lawrence Lambert, Caroline Guthrie (courting couple) Robert Stephens (Ted, the drunk), Timothy Chaplin (youth in pub), Nick Edmett, David Finch, Mark Long, Tommy Wright (working men in pub), Leonard Kirby (young fan), Sean O'Bryan (Lewis Seeley), Debra Maria Moore (Lita Grey), Donald Elson (prop man), Donnie Kehr (Joe, sound engineer), Sky Rumph (Charles Chaplin Jr. aged 7), Bradley Pierce (Sydney Chaplin Jr, aged 6), Richard James (pianist at Perrino's), William Dennis Hunt (Maitre d' at Perrino's), Michael Blevins (David Raksin), Michael Goorjian (Charles Chaplin Jr), Michael Cade (Sydney Chaplin Jr), Norbert Weisser (German diplomat), Vicki Frederick, Gene Wolande, Michael Adler, Iris Bath, Thomas K. Belgrey, Tom Preston, Mary Stark, Annie Waterman (guests at Pebble Beach party), Quinn Harmon (make-up girl), Michael Eugene Fairman (assistant director), Robert Peters (camera operator), Noah Margetts (clapper boy), Jodi Carlisle (script girl), Rhett Smith (tennis party guest), John Standing (Chaplin butler in Hollywood), Jennifer Whitlock (studio secretary), Todd Mason Covert, Phil Forman, Charley J. Garrett, Jerry Giles, Howard Hughes, Jayson Kane, Michael Miller, John Otrin, J. Michael Patterson, Paul Sinclair, Terrence Stone, Ralph Votrian (reporters at Los Angeles Theatre), 'Aggie' Aguilar (officer on 'Queen Elizabeth'), Emma Lewis (production assistant at Academy Awards), Lachele Carl (chorus girl), Barry McCarthy (TV technician).

13,035 ft. 145 mins

Shadowlands   GB   1993

D: Richard Attenborough. sc: William Nicholson. dist: UIP. pc: Shadowlands Productions/Spelling Films International in association with Price Entertainments/Savoy Pictures. exec p: Terence Clegg. p: Richard Attenborough. Brian Eastman. co-p: Diana Hawkins. ass.p: Alison Webb. p.co-ordinator: Leila Kirkpatrick. location managers: Nicholas Daubeny,

Richard Dunmore. Casting: Lucy Boulting. ass.d: Patrick Clayton, Michael Stevenson, Sean Clayton. 2nd unit: Adam Sommer. dir.ph: Roger Pratt; scope, colour. 2nd unit dir.ph: Eddie Collins. cam. op: Michael Roberts. 2nd unit: Martin Kenzie. plate ph and Translites: Alan White. optical and digital effects: Peerless Camera Company. editor: Lesley Walker. prod.des: Stuart Craig. sup.a.d: John King. art dir: Michael Lamont. set decorator: Stephenie McMillan. draughtsman: Peter Dorme; junior: Paul Kirby. scenic artist: Brian Bishop. storyboard artist: Tony Wright. special effects supervisor: Chris Corbould. special effects: Brian Warner. music/music director: George Fenton. music performed by The London Symphony Orchestra, The Choir of Magdalen College, Oxford. soloists: Daniel Cochin, Daren Geraghty. music editor: Kevin Lane. music co-ordinator: Eliza Thompson. costume design: Penny Rose. wardrobe superviser: Kenny Crouch. make-up design: Christine Beveridge. make-up artist: Norma Webb. hairdresser: Betty Glasgow. title design: Barbra Flinder. dialogue editor: Michael Crouch. Foley editor: Peter Holt. sound rec: Simon Kaye, Jonathan Bates, Gerry Humphreys; mus: Keith Grant. Dolby stereo. sound re-recordists: Dean Humphreys. ADR/Foley: John Bateman.
CAST: Anthony Hopkins (Jack Lewis), Debra Winger (Joy Gresham), John Wood (Christopher Riley), Edward Hardwicke (Warnie Lewis), Joseph Mazzello (Douglas Gresham), Julian Fellowes (Desmond Arding), Roddy Maude-Roxby (Arnold Dopliss), Michael Denison (Harry Harrington), Peter Firth (Doctor Craig), Andrew Seear (Bob Chafer), Tim McMullan (Nick Farrell), Andrew Hawkins (Rupert Parrish), Peter Howell (College President), Robert Fie (Claude Bird), James Frain (Peter Whistler), Toby Whithouse (Frith), Daniel Goode (Lieven), Scott Handy (Standish), Charles Simon (Barker), Giles Oldershaw (Marcus), Simon Cowell-Parker (John Egan), Roger Ashton-Griffiths (Doctor Eddie Monk), Pat Keen (Mrs Young), Carol Passmore (Woman in Tea Room), Howard 'Lew' Lewis (Tea Room Waiter), Jan Quentin (Station Acquaintance), Alan Talbot (College Porter), Leigh Burton-Gill (Mrs Parrish), Cameron Burton-Gill, Chandler Burton-Gill, Kendall Burton-Gill, Christina Burton-Gill (Parrish Children), Sylvia Barter (Woman in Bookshop), James Watt (Boy in Bookshop), Pauline Melville (Committee Chairwoman), Sophie Stanton, Ysobel Gonzalez, Ninka Scott (Lecture Committee), Walter Sparrow (Fred Paxford), Gerald Sim (Superintendent Registrar), Terry Rowley (Registrar), Norman Bird (Taxi Driver Witness), Abigail Harrison (Staff Nurse), Julian Firth (Father John Fisher), Karen Lewis (Hotel Receptionist), Matthew Delamere (Simon Chadwick). 11,803 ft. 131 mins

In Love and War   USA   1996

d: Richard Attenborough. sc: Allan Scott, Clancy Sigal, Hamilton Phelan. screen story: Allan Scott, Dimitri Villard, based on the book by Henry S. Villard and James Nagel. p.c: New Line Productions, in association with Dimitri Villard Productions. exec.p: Sara Risher. p: Dimitri Villard, Richard Attenborough. Supervising p: Chris Kenny. co-p: Diana Hawkins. ass.p: Janis Rothbard Chaskin. prod. exec: A. J. Cohen. prod.ass: Judy Wasdell. executive in charge of production: Carla Fry. production co-ordinators: Leila Kirkpatrick; in-house: Emily Glatter; Italian unit, Caterina Zerbini; Canadian unit: Helene Ross. unit prod. managers: Judi Bunn; Italian unit: Guido Cerasuolo; Canadian unit: Richard Lalonde. unit manager: Canadian unit: Mario Nadeau. location managers: Hugh Harlow; Italian unit: Enrico Ballarin, Luisa Amendola; Italian 2nd Unit: Ladis Zanini.

executive in charge of post-production: Joe Fineman. 2nd unit director: Arthur Wooster. ass. dirs: Patrick Clayton, Michael Stevenson, Sean Clayton, Ian Stone; 2nd unit: Terry Madden, Jerry Daly; Italian unit: Luca Lachin, Pierantonio Novara; Canadian unit: Normand Labelle, Marie-Josée Leroux, Robert Cote. script superviser: Nikki Clapp; 2nd unit: Suzanne Clegg. casting: Jeremy Zimmerman, René Haynes, Clare Walker; Montreal: Elite Productions. d.ph: Roger Pratt. Eastmancolor. cam.ops: Simon Ransley; 2nd Unit: Tim Wooster. visual effects: The Magic Camera Company; supervisor: Antony Hunt; motion control cameraman: Riek Mietkowski; motion control technician: Andrew Stevens; digital artists: Angus Cameron, Daniel Pettipher, Helen Ball, Roger Gibbon. graphic artist Canadian unit: Denis Caspar. special effects co-ordinator: Richard Conway. senior technicians: Tim Willis, Dave Eltham; Italian unit supervisor: Raffaele Battistelli. editor Lesley Walker. prod. des:Stuart Craig. supervising art director: Neil Lamont. art directors: John King, Michael Lamont; Italian unit: Aurelio Crugnola; Canadian unit: Guy Lalande. set decorators Stephenie McMillan; Canadian unit: Ann Galéa, Pierre L'Heureux. scenic artists: Brian Bishop, Doug Bishop. storyboard artist: Denis Rich. sculptor: Andrew Holder. costume designer: Penny Rose. wardrobe supervisor: Anne Crawford; Supervisor - Canadian unit: Francesca Chamberland; master: Mark Holmes; master – Italy: Gorden Harmer; mistress: Sue Honeyborne. chief hairdresser: Lisa Tomblin. hairdressers: Hilary Haines; Canadian Unit: André Duval, Raymond Laliberté. make-up chief: Daniel Parker. make-up artists: Sallie Evans, Jeremy Woodhead; 2nd Unit: Trefor Proud, Wanda Kelly; Canadian unit: Christiane Fattori, Camille Belanger, Alex Lambert. prosthetics: Jeremy Woodhead. title design:Chris Allies. title illustrations: John Rose. titles:

The Magic Camera Company. music/music conductor/orchestrations: George Fcnton. orchestrations: Simon Chamberlain, Geoffrey Alexander. orchestra leader: Gavyn Wright. music co-ordinators: Eliza Thompson; New Line Cinema: Mark Kaufman. music editor: Kevin Lane. recording engineer: Keith Grant. song 'Beer Barrel Polka' by Lew Brown, Wladimir A. Timm, Jaromir Vejvoda, Vasek Zeman. sd: Simon Kaye, Jonathan Bates, Gerry Humphreys. sd. mixers: Dean Humphreys, Tim Cavagin; 2nd unit: David Allen. dialogue eds:Mike Crouch; 2nd unit: Roy Burge. ADR mixer: John Bateman. Foley artist: Pauline Griffiths; mixer: John Baternan; ed: Peter Holt. military advisers: Italian unit: Lt Colonel Lorenzo Cadedau, Captain Jean Claude Ritacca. stunt co-ordinator: Eddie Stacey. supervising armourer: Carl Schmidt. armourer:Italian unit: Paolo Del Bravo. animal wrangler: Tony Doyle.

CAST: Sandra Bullock (Agnes von Kurowsky), Chris O'Donnell (Ernest Hemingway), Mackenzie Astin (Henry Villard) Emilio Bonucci (Domenico Caracciolo), Ingrid Lamy (Elsie 'Mac' MacDonald), Margot Steinberg (Mabel 'Rosie' Rose), Tara Hugo (Katherine 'Gumshoe' DeLong), Colin Stinton (Tom Burnside), Rocco Quarzell (Roberto Zardini), Ian Kelly (Jimmy McBride), Vincenzo Nicoli (Enrico Biscaglia) Allan Bennett, Terence Sach (porters), Carlo Croccolo (town mayor) Gigi Vivan (Italian child), Giuseppe Donato (grandfather), Allegro Di Carpegna (Loretta Cavanaugh), Diane Witter (Adele Brown), Mindy Lee Raskin (Charlotte Anne Miller), Tracy Hostmyer (Ruth Harper) Kaethe Cherney (Veta Markley), Lauren Booth (Anna Scanlon), Rebecca Craig (Elena Crouch), Frances Riddelle (Katherine Smith), Wendi Peters (Emily Rahn), Laura Hardi (Teresa), Maria Petrucci (Sonia), Valeria Fabbri (Anna Maria) Quinto Rolman (Italian man), Ralph Taylor

(Francesco), George Rossi (Triage medic), Todd Curran (Skip Talbot), Matthew Sharp (Joseph Larkin), Mick Brooks (Louis Burton) Tom Goodman-Hill (Houston Kenyon), Doreen Mantle (Emilia), Tim McDonell (adjutant), Vincenzo Ricotta (Italian officer) Reno Porcaro (Italian photographer), Bruno Majean (Alberto Zardini), Joseph Long (Italian doctor), Bruce Lidington (American surgeon), Colin Fox (Dr Hemingway), Kay Hawtrey (Grace Hemingway), Roseline Garland (Carol Hemingway), Ivan Smirnow (Leicester Hemingway), Avery Saltzman (Oak Leaves reporter), Rodger Battue (Sun-Times reporter), Richard Blackburn (Tribune reporter), Gil Filar, Noah Reid (boys), Richard Fitzpatrick (mailman), Philippe Leroy (Count Sergio Caracciolo) Laura Martelli (Isabella Caracciolo), Cyril Taylor (maitre d'), Milan Rosandic (waiter) 19,393 ft. 114 mins 29 secs

Grey Owl   USA   1999

D: Richard Attenborough. sc: Willliam Nicholson. pc: Beaver Productions Ltd. p: Richard Attenborough, Jake Eberts, Claude Léger. Assoc.p: Diana Hawkins. exec p: Barr B.Potter, Lenny Young Line p: Josette Perrotta ph: Roger Pratt. ed: Lesley Walker. Casting: Rene Haynes, Vera Miller, Nadia Rona. Prod des: Anthony Pratt. a.d: Claude Paré. Set dec: Bruno Sorel, Joanne Woollard. Cost: Renée April. Mus: George Fenton

CAST: Pierce Brosnan (Archie Grey Owl), Stewart Bick (Cyrus Finney), Vlasta Vrana (Harry Champlin), Annie Galipeau (Pony), Neil Kroetsch (First Hunter), Serge Houe, (Second Hunter), Peter Colvey (Hotel Guest), Nathaniel Arcand (Ned White Bear), Jacques Lussier (Manager), Lee-Roy Jacobs (Hotel Porter),

Jimmy Herman (Chief Pete Misebi), John Dunn-Hill (Sim Hancock), Graham Greene (Jim Bernard), Gordon Masten (Gus Mitchell), Chip Chuipka (First Trapper), John Walsh (Second Trapper), David Fox (Jim Wood), Annabelle Torsein, Marcel Jeannin, Kent McQuaid, Craig Gautier (Hikers), Matthew Sharp (Hiker Hawkins), Charles Powell (Walter Perry), Sean Gallagher (Bill Oliver), James Bradford (Tom Walker), Nöel Burton (Southampton Reporter), Renée Asherson (Carrie Belaney), Stephanie Cole (Ada Belaney), Richard Jutras, Art Kitching, Pierre Lenoir , Norris Domingue (Halifax Reporters), Al Vandercruys (Immigration Officer), Floyd 'Red Crow' Westerman (Pow Wow Chief), Saginaw Grant (Pow Wow Chief), Gene Blackbird, Lindsey Cote, Arnold Jocks, Takatie Montour, Rene Tonda Splicer Kiepprien, Donald J.White, Kevin Peltier, Donald Swamp (Wabiken Lodge Dancers), Gerald McDonald (Lead Wabiken Lodge Drummer), Michael MacDonald, Narcisse Kagebabon (Wabiken Lodge Drummers), Timothy Eashappie (Lead Pow Wow Dancer), Frank Buswa, Vernon Cardinal, Josie Cox, Donald Dowd, Hilliard Friday, Les Harper, David Herman, Joseph McLeod, Dylan Manitopyes, Brian Moore, Gordie Odjig, Gary Parker, Ron Ranville, Steve Sands, Dwight 'Bucko' Teeple, Denis Whiteye, larry Yazzie (Pow Wow Dancers) Steve Wood (Lead Pow Wow Drummer), Elmer Baptiste, Shane Dion, Aaron McGilvery, Bradley McGilvery, Ferlin McGilvery, Cecil Nepoose, Leroy Whitstone (Pow Wow Drummers), , Jeffrey Lee (Chief's Counselman – uncredited), King George VI, Queen Elizabeth, Queen Elizabeth II, as Princess Elizabeth, Princess Margaret (themselves, in archive footage) 10, 641 ft. 118 Mins